Essential cataloguing

Essential cataloguing

J. H. Bowman

facet publishing

Published by Facet Publishing,
7 Ridgmount Street, London WC1E 7AE
www.facetpublishing.co.uk

Facet Publishing is wholly owned by CILIP: the Chartered Institute of
Library and Information Professionals.

First published 2003
Reprinted 2003, 2004, 2005, 2006, 2007 (with corrections), 2008, 2009

British Library Cataloguing in Publication Data
A catalogue record for this book is available from the British Library.

ISBN 978-1-85604-456-1

Typeset in Plantin and Gill Sans by Facet Publishing.
Printed and made in the United Kingdom by MPG Books Group Ltd,
Bodmin, Cornwall.

Contents

Acknowledgements

I am grateful to my colleague Vanda Broughton and to Robert Atkinson, sometime chief cataloguer at University College London, each of whom read a draft of the text and made valuable comments. It hardly needs adding that neither is responsible for the errors that the book inevitably contains.

Every effort has been made to trace the holders of copyright in the title pages reproduced. I thank the following publishers for permission to reproduce title pages and other elements from their books:

(Fig. 4.1) B. T. Batsford; (Fig. 4.2) reprinted from *The natural history of moles*, by M. L. Gorman and R. D. Stone, copyright 1990, with permission from Elsevier Science; (Fig. 4.3) University of Oklahoma Press; (Fig. 4.4) John W. Trimmer; (Fig. 4.5) Souvenir Press; (Fig. 4.6) HarperCollins © 1993 Henry Beard; (Fig. 4.7) Oxford University Press (East Asia); (Fig. 4.9) Random House UK; (Fig. 4.10) reprinted by permissions from *Melancholies of knowledge: literature in the age of science* by Margery Arent Safir (ed.), the State University of New York Press ©1999 State University of New York. All Rights Reserved; (Fig. 4.11) Cheshire Community Council; (Fig. 4.13) reprinted from *Bird census techniques* by Colin Bibby et al., copyright 2000, with permission from Elsevier Science; (Fig. 4.14) from Fenwick, H., *Q & A constitutional and administrative law*, 2nd edn, 1995 (4th edn, 2003), London: Cavendish Publishing; (Fig. 4.15) Transworld Publishers; (Fig. 4.16) from *Winfield on tort* by Winfield and Jolowicz, Sweet & Maxwell, 1994; (Fig. 4.17) London Assembly; (Fig. 4.18 and Fig. 5.3) Thomas Telford Publishing; (Fig. 5.1) International Society for Horticultural Science; (Fig. 5.2) American Mathematical Society; (Fig. 5.5 and Fig. 5.6) HMSO; (Fig. 5.7) *16th International Seaweed Symposium*, with kind permission of Kluwer Academic Publishers; (Fig. 5.8) Flavia de Grey; (Fig. 5.9) British Museum Press; (Fig. 5.10) *Winward Fearon on collateral warranties* by D. L. Cornes and R. Winward, Blackwell Science; (Fig. 5.11) Macmillan Education; (Fig. 5.12) N. Pevsner, *London 1: The cities of London and Westminster*, 3rd ed., © 1973, Yale University Press; (Fig. 5.13) from *The Freedom of Information Act*, LexisNexis Butterworths Tolley; (Fig. 5.14) Thames & Hudson; (Fig. 5.15) Findhorn Press; (Fig. 6.1) Random House; (Fig. 6.2) Gordon Campbell (ed.), *The*

Renaissance, 1989, Macmillan Education, reproduced with permission of Palgrave; (Fig. 6.3) Oxford English dictionary additions series: Volume one edited by Simpson and Weiner (1993), reprinted by permission of Oxford University Press; (Fig. 8.1) *Advances in artificial intelligence*, 1998 © Springer-Verlag; (Figs. 9.1–9.5) Library of Congress; (Fig. 10.1) Verso Publishers; (Fig. 10.2) *Robinson Crusoe* (Oxford world's classics) by Daniel Defoe (1999), reprinted by permission of Oxford University Press; (Fig. 10.3) taken from *NIV study Bible* (fully revised). Copyright 1985, 1987, 2002 by Zondervan NIV text: 1973, 1978, 1984 by International Bible Society. Used by permission of Zondervan; (Fig. 10.4) John Betjeman, *Collected poems*, John Murray (Publishers) Ltd.

1 Introduction

The aim of this book

If you are looking at this book it may be because you are interested in cataloguing. If you are not, I hope that by reading it you will find that cataloguing is not as bad as you thought.

The book is written with three main kinds of reader in mind:

- library school students
- beginning cataloguers
- other information professionals who have forgotten all they ever knew about cataloguing but now find that they have to do it.

If you fall into one of these categories, I hope that you will find something useful in this book, as I take you through the various processes which are involved in cataloguing using AACR2. I must emphasize at the outset that

- it is not intended as a substitute for AACR2; indeed I assume throughout that you have a copy of AACR2 with you while you read it
- it does not purport to cover everything in AACR2. I have tried to give you the basics, but without completely eliminating some of the difficult decision-making which makes up much of cataloguing
- it is intended to be essentially practical. This means that although there is some background material it does not amount to much, and you should refer to other books such as Oddy (1996) and Piggott (1988) for further background information.

Layout

Information about MARC coding is in the left-hand margin.

To make it easier for you to stick to the essentials, two sizes of type are used.

References to AACR2 rule numbers are in the right-hand margin.

The most important parts are set like this.

The less important parts are set like this.

```
Examples look like this.
```

Non-book materials

You will probably think that this book concentrates rather too much on books. Perhaps it does, but it is much easier to reproduce the relevant parts of books. Moreover, when it comes to cataloguing, most libraries are still dealing largely with books.

I believe that if you understand the principles of cataloguing you should be able to transfer them to all kinds of material without too much difficulty. I have included references to some of the non-book materials which libraries are most likely to encounter, and they are shown like this.

And every so often there are summaries of key points in boxes like this.

The need for cataloguing

Cataloguing has long been unpopular, and nowadays is little taught. Ever since computers began to be used in cataloguing (see p. 9) there has been a school of thought that in some mysterious way computers would be able to do all the cataloguing that was necessary, and that it would no longer be necessary to employ human cataloguers.

It is true that catalogue records can now be copied and shared in a way that was not previously possible, but this has not eliminated the need for cataloguers. Far from it: with the increasing use of computerized catalogues it has become necessary to convert the older card catalogues into computerized form, and many cataloguers are needed for this.

Another fallacy about cataloguing is this: that it is simply a matter of following rules without using any thought. This implies that very little training is required for cataloguers, and that cataloguers can therefore be employed on very low salary grades.

This too is quite unjustified. While it is important to follow the rules (because otherwise there is no point in having them), many of them require *flexibility* and *discretion*. This does *not* mean that you may break the rules when you do not agree with them; you may not. But it does mean that you will encounter numerous situations where the rules do not tell you exactly what to do, and you have to use your discretion.

A further misconception is that somehow cataloguing rules are the province of cataloguers only, and that other librarians and information professionals need know nothing about them. This is a quite misguided point of view. All library professionals are presumably there with the main purpose of helping their users find the materials they are looking for. How can they do this if they do not understand the rules and principles on which the catalogue is based?

Many aspects of cataloguing rules are obscure, and you cannot expect catalogue users to understand them – or even know them. Some of them are positively unhelpful. It is therefore the duty of all librarians to know what the main problems are likely to be, so as to be able to interpret the catalogue to its users. It is not acceptable just to say: 'Oh, that's nothing to do with me; blame the cataloguers'.

What makes a good cataloguer?

The main thing is to have a sense of humour. You will have to apply rules which you find quite silly, and you cannot really take them all seriously. On a scale of the world's problems cataloguing would not feature at all. However, *you must pretend to take them seriously*, and pretend, while you are doing it, that cataloguing is the most important thing in the world. You must regard every decision, as well as every full stop and comma, as being of vital importance.

This is because the other chief attribute that you need is attention to detail. Carelessness will not do. It is just as easy to do something properly as to do it wrong, and so you should decide at the outset that you are going to be one of those people who do it properly. You will not be one who writes 'forward' when the book says 'foreword', or 'organisation' when the title has 'organization'. You will thrill to the difference between the abbreviations 'no' and 'no.'. If you are not prepared to make the effort then you are not suited to being a cataloguer.

Cataloguing *is* important. It is the principal means whereby library users can find the contents of the collection. Now that most cataloguing is computerized, it is even more important to avoid errors, because a simple mistake can make a catalogue record – and therefore an item – irretrievable.

I have tried to include a reasonable number of illustrations in the book and, although it has not been possible in every case, my aim has been to provide something both to amuse and to illuminate. All the examples are genuine, and I hope that they will help you to appreciate that cataloguing can be fun – really.

2 Background to cataloguing and AACR2

This book is designed to help you to use AACR2. But in order to put cataloguing into context it may be useful for you to read this background chapter. If you are really keen to get straight to the practical cataloguing, then by all means skip it.

What is a catalogue?

If you ask someone this, with no particular context, I am sure that the average person will have a mental picture of the answer. It will probably not include a library catalogue, but is more likely to be a catalogue of goods available in a shop or on mail order, such as the Argos catalogue. The mental image will probably be of some *specific physical form*, perhaps a large paperback book.

In a library context, the physical form of the catalogue is not particularly important. Most present-day catalogues are online, and this makes them far more comparable than they were previously to online information retrieval systems, or to search engines on the world wide web. Online catalogues are likely to continue for the foreseeable future, but in the past there have been printed catalogues, card catalogues, slip catalogues and various microform catalogues, film or fiche. An online catalogue is now usually known as an OPAC (Online Public Access Catalogue), and normally gives a far wider range of access points (ways of looking things up) than any of the previous forms.

Many of the cataloguing rules that we follow today were designed for older physical forms of catalogue, where the labour of providing multiple access points would have been such that they had to be strictly limited. You might feel that some of these rules are now outdated, and you would be right. The fact is, however, that AACR2 still contains them, and this book is based on AACR2. So you will just have to follow them!

Why have catalogues?

It would be an unusual library that had no catalogue of any kind. One reason to have a catalogue is the inventorial, i.e. simply to keep a record of what has been acquired. Some libraries still maintain an *accessions register*, which just lists brief details of all the items acquired, in the order in which they are received.

The main reason, though, for having a catalogue is to allow the library's users to find the items they want in the library. To amplify this we still cannot do much better than quote Cutter, who wrote the following in 1876 (Cutter 1904, 12):

1. To enable a person to find a book of which either
   (A) the author
   (B) the title   }   is known.
   (C) the subject
2. To show what the library has
   (D) by a given author
   (E) on a given subject
   (F) in a given kind of literature.
3. To assist in the choice of a book
   (G) as to its edition (bibliographically)
   (H) as to its character (literary or topical).

In Britain, some of these purposes were not properly fulfilled until the advent of the OPAC. For example, it was unusual to provide title access in many catalogues, and users were expected to know the authors of the works they required. In the USA a much more approachable system operated, with author, title and subject entries all interfiled in what is known as a *dictionary catalogue*. Now that most libraries have OPACs it has become much easier to provide a greater variety of access points.

What is cataloguing?

Cataloguing can be divided into several functions, and to some extent the terminology is ambiguous. The first great division is into

- descriptive cataloguing
- subject cataloguing.

Descriptive cataloguing (in this sense) means describing the item, and allocating the access points to it *that have nothing to do with its subject matter*.

Subject cataloguing itself comprises two main aspects:

- classification
- subject headings.

There are several general classification schemes and numerous specialized ones in use, and various different systems of subject headings. Most libraries have some form of classified shelf-arrangement, and many use subject headings, but neither of these things is covered in this book. This book is about *descriptive cataloguing* only.

Descriptive cataloguing itself can, however, be broken down into more than one aspect:

- description
- access points.

The book is concerned entirely with these and they will be explained in detail. But it will be useful if you can understand the difference now.

- **Description**
  You describe the item (book, video, web page, etc.), by *copying out* its title, showing who published it and how long it is, etc.
  At this stage you are *not* concerned with how users might be able to look it up in the catalogue.
- **Access points**
  You make access points (entry points) which will allow users to find the item in the catalogue.

The whole structure of AACR2 is based on this division into two processes, and so it is important to understand it. The older cataloguing codes did not make the distinction so clearly, because it had not been properly thought of in those days. They tended to treat description and access points as very much interrelated.

It is perhaps not surprising that the distinction had not been thought of. I suspect that most ordinary people would not think of it. If I gave you a shelfful of books and asked you to make a *list* of them, what would you do? How would you write them down? I imagine that you would include the title of each of them, and perhaps the author. But I guarantee that you would not write the author's name down *twice*, just because it appears after the title on the title page *and* you want to list it at the start of your entry. Yet this is what AACR2 requires you to do, because description and access points are quite separate things.

The importance of catalogues

Why are catalogues important? Why do they matter? They are important because they provide a systematic means of retrieval of items in a collection, and because they bring order to the arrangement of that collection.

The catalogue itself should also be orderly. Its arrangement should be clear and logical, and it should be easy to understand its structure and its displays. Inconsistency within a catalogue, though it usually occurs, should really be avoided by all possible means.

Main and added entries

Going back to the imaginary shelfful of books, what if one of them had two authors? I am quite certain that you would not list the book twice, once under each author. No normal booklist or bibliography would do this, because they work on the *single entry* principle.

But this is where a catalogue differs from just any list. It is usual to make extra entries – called *added entries* – where more than one author is involved, and indeed in all sorts of other cases too, as we shall see.

It is this potential conflict between the single entry principle and the provision of multiple entries that gives rise to the distinction between main and added entries which is still fundamental to AACR2 today. In the days when most catalogues were produced manually, or by printing from type, it was expensive to produce more than one entry for the same item. Many libraries therefore gave the full details of the item in one place only (the main entry) and made the added entry little more (sometimes no more) than a cross-reference to the main entry. This allowed additional authors to be found, but if you wanted to see the full details of the item you had to look at the main entry.

Now that most catalogues are online, the cost of providing extra access points is negligible, and all of them act equally as pointers to the same descriptive record.

Because of this, there have been many proposals over the years to abolish the distinction between main and added entries and to make all access points the same, but so far they have come to nothing. In practice, in an OPAC it does not matter what kind of entry point you search under because they will all lead you to the full catalogue record, which means that most catalogue users will be unaware of any distinction. AACR2, however, maintains the distinction, and we must therefore observe it in this book.

Origins of modern cataloguing

Bearing in mind the distinction between descriptive cataloguing and access points, we can trace the origins of the current AACR2 code to the early 1950s. At that time there was some dissatisfaction with the then widely used code which dated back to 1908 (Library Association

1908), and at the Library of Congress Seymour Lubetzky was asked to look at the problems. As a result of his work (Lubetzky 1953) an International Committee of Cataloguing Experts was set up, and this committee organized an International Conference on Cataloguing Principles, which was held in Paris in 1961. It was on the recommendations of this conference that the first edition of AACR in 1967 was based, as far as access points and forms of name were concerned.

The description aspect of cataloguing – that is, what elements should be included in the description, and the order in which they should occur – had always been rather neglected. It was perhaps assumed that a cataloguer would copy out the necessary information to form a description without too much specific guidance. The Library of Congress had its own guidance, which supplemented the published cataloguing codes, and in due course attention was directed to this at an international level and a series of meetings was held in 1969 to consider it.

International Standard Bibliographic Description

The result of this was the development of International Standard Bibliographic Description (ISBD). After some preliminary drafts the first standard ISBD was published in 1974 (*ISBD(M): international standard bibliographic description for monographic publications*) and since then there have been many others, catering for different formats of publication. ISBD deals with the description aspect of cataloguing only, *not* with access points or forms of name. It lays down, for each physical form of publication:

- the sources of information to be used as the basis for the description
- the order in which the elements must be transcribed
- the punctuation that should be used to separate the elements.

The aims of ISBD are

- to help make catalogue records more interchangeable between countries, so that libraries can use each other's records more easily
- to assist in interpreting catalogue records across language barriers
- to assist in converting records to machine-readable form.

Punctuation

You might think that punctuation is a strange thing to include in a standard for descriptive cataloguing. Certainly, prior to ISBD, very little guidance was provided and cataloguers would follow their own local rules for punctuation.

The useful thing about it is that it helps you to see the elements of the catalogue record more clearly. It is related to the second of the aims just mentioned, because even if you cannot read the language it should help you to make out where one part of a catalogue record finishes and another begins, by looking at the punctuation around the sequence of elements. Punctuation is now a fundamental feature of AACR2, and if you are going to follow AACR2 properly you will need to get to grips with it.

Standards

The first edition of AACR in 1967 was of course too early to be influenced by ISBD, but the second edition in 1978 reflected its influence and was closely, though not absolutely, based on it. This is particularly apparent in the rules regarding the sources of information to be used in the description, the order of the elements, and the punctuation to be used between them. The adoption of AACR2 and the spread of the MARC format have both led to a much greater degree of standardization in cataloguing than previously existed.

Why is standardization so important? There are several reasons, which are interrelated.

In the first place, it seems sensible that libraries which acquire the same items should be able to copy each other's catalogue records rather than each producing identical records individually. This is obviously only attainable if they are following the same codes and using the same structures.

Secondly, it benefits library users if they find that catalogues in different institutions are compiled in the same way. They do not have to learn a new system to use a different catalogue.

The prime reason, however, is economic. Ever since the Library of Congress started its printed card service in 1901 it has been possible for libraries to buy in their catalogue records rather than having to create all their own. In Britain there was no comparable service until 1956, when the British National Bibliography started to issue printed cards (Stephens 1994, 19), but with the advent of computerization in the 1960s it became much easier to obtain records from external sources.

The advent of computerization has also made cooperation and record-sharing much easier. Although cooperative systems had existed in different ways for a long time, it was not until the development of the MARC format in the 1960s that they really developed. OCLC Online Computer Library Center started in 1967 as a local arrangement in Ohio, and from that has grown to become the world's largest co-operative cataloguing agency.

Clearly the benefit of obtaining records from elsewhere is greatly reduced if a library finds that it has to make many alterations to the records it receives. This means that although in the past many libraries maintained that their users were special in some way and therefore had special needs with regard to catalogue records, these largely imaginary needs have now been quietly abandoned so that as many libraries as possible can benefit from using the same catalogue records.

Having records in a standard format is also very important from the point of view of automated library management systems. Assuming that you have an automated system it is likely that every few years you will need to upgrade the system or undertake a system migration, choosing a quite different system. The existence of uniform standards, and the MARC format, makes this very much easier than if you are using a format which is unique to your particular system. The system supplier knows what to expect of the format and the transition is likely to go much more smoothly.

Finally, there is perhaps an idealistic reason for standardization, though this is harder to define. But for well over a century there has been a dream that it might be possible to compile a world bibliography. This is unlikely ever to be attainable, but standardization of catalogue records is certainly a means to that end.

I recognize that nowadays most cataloguers probably obtain the majority of their records from external sources, but *someone* has to create those records and perhaps that someone is you. The purpose of this book is therefore to help you with creating records from scratch.

MARC

MARC stands for MAchine Readable Catalog(u)ing. The idea of using computers to speed up catalogue production goes back to the 1950s but it was not until 1965 that MARC came into being. It started as a pilot project at the Library of Congress, and was soon followed by a similar project in the UK, organized by the Council of the British National Bibliography (Ilill 1999, 3).

In 1968 these two projects came together to form MARC II, which was an Anglo-American attempt to produce a standard version of the format. The aims of MARC from the outset were that it should be

- usable for all kinds of library materials, not just books
- usable in automated library systems

- flexible enough for use in a variety of applications, not just catalogue production.

During succeeding years two main versions of the format were developed: UK MARC in the UK and USMARC in the USA. The variations between them were due to the different requirements of the controlling bodies.

By the 1990s there were nearly 50 different MARC formats in use in different countries, all largely based on either the American or the British original. It was realized that it would be highly desirable if these variations could be reconciled and eventually brought back together, and after long deliberation and consultation the British Library in 2001 decided to discontinue use of its own format, UK MARC, and adopt the Library of Congress version, which in 1998 had been renamed MARC 21.

The main features of MARC are described in the next chapter (pp. 16–19).

3 Structure of AACR2 and of the MARC 21 format

AACR2 divides cataloguing into the two main processes that I mentioned on p. 6:

- description
- access points.

The arrangement of the code depends on this basic distinction.

The whole of AACR2 Part I covers description. Because of the way the chapters are laid out there is considerable repetition, and it is usually necessary to look at two chapters at the same time.

This is because Chapter 1 is written in very general terms. It is intended to apply to any kind of material that might need to be catalogued: it is not specifically about books, or videos, or electronic resources, or anything else. But because these specific formats – and the rest – each have unique features they need chapters of their own, to elaborate on Chapter 1 and to give more specific examples.

In order to avoid too much repetition, each of Chapters 2–12 keeps referring back to Chapter 1, and *uses the same numbering system for its sections*. This means that once you know that section .4 of Chapter 1 refers to the Publication, distribution, etc., area of the description, you automatically know that section .4 of Chapter 7 will refer to the Publication, distribution, etc., area for videorecordings.

AACR2 Chapter 13 is an exception to this scheme. It does not follow the same arrangement as Chapters 1–12, but deals solely with the making of analytical entries.

The **access points** aspect of cataloguing can be further broken down, as follows:

- **Selection of access point**
  For example, in cataloguing an edition of *Macbeth*, who is the author? Answer: Shakespeare, but at this stage we are not concerned about how to spell his name.
- **Selection of name to be used as basis for heading**
  Continuing with the same example, although there was a long period

when the spelling 'Shakspere' was common, we shall use the form 'William Shakespeare' because that is how his name is usually spelt nowadays. Note that in choosing this form we may be departing from the form that appears in the item itself.

- **Construction of heading**

  What order should we use for the elements of the name 'William Shakespeare'? In introducing ourselves we usually use our names in *direct order* (I would say that I am John Bowman) but in alphabetical lists different languages and countries have different systems. We expect to find English names under surname, with other elements inverted, which means that the form of name for Shakespeare would be 'Shakespeare, William'.

In reality it is unlikely that many cataloguers strictly separate the different processes of description and access points in the way that AACR2 suggests. Most books (and many other items) are so straightforward that it is perfectly obvious what the access points are going to be from the moment you see the item.

Nevertheless, it is useful at least to pretend to adopt this method because it forces you to look at the two aspects separately. In this way you will not be tempted to let one influence the other. It can also be quite comforting when confronted with something that you cannot understand, because you can always start by copying out the title.

There is one exception: when you are copying out the title you may find that it contains the name of a corporate body, which includes conferences. In English, such a name will have Capital Letters for the Main Words. As we shall see later (p. 92) the decision as to whether a conference has a name can be less than straightforward, but until you have made this decision you will not be able to copy out the title correctly.

When considering the name to be used as the basis for a heading, in the vast majority of cases there is likewise no difficulty because the person or organization concerned has only ever used one form of name. But the rules have to cater for the more difficult cases as well.

Appendices

The rest of AACR2 consists of appendices, which deal with

A Capitalization
B Abbreviations
C Numerals
D Glossary
E Initial articles

I recommend you to have a good look through Appendices A, B and C so that you know what kinds of thing they cover.

As we shall see as we go along, you will find that the rules on capitalization are very detailed, and it is important to know the basics of what they contain. Similarly, only the authorized abbreviations are allowed to be used – and then *only when specifically instructed* in particular areas of the description – but when they are allowed they are compulsory, which means that again you need to be familiar with them.

App. A

App. B

If during the course of using AACR2 you come across a term that you don't understand, you should be able to find it in Appendix D.

App. D

The general introduction
There are a few sections here which are particularly useful. Some of them give very important information which is not repeated elsewhere in AACR2.

Main and added entries

0.5

I have already mentioned (p. 7) the question of main and added entries. This section gives AACR2's justification for continuing with this distinction, namely that it is useful for

- making a single entry listing; or
- for making a single citation to another work.

It is the second of these that is sometimes puzzling. The kind of situation it refers to is when, in cataloguing one item, you find that you need to mention another, perhaps because one is a sequel to another, or an index to it, or has some other relationship to it. In these cases it is useful to have a standard form of citing the item.

The idea that main entries have any bearing on bibliographical citation is quite fanciful. There are many different styles for bibliographic citation, and any resemblance they bear to AACR2 is entirely accidental.

Structure of entries

0.6

It is easy to forget this rule, and if you are using an automated catalogue you have no reason to look at it at all, because the system will do the work for you, and probably in a different way. It simply tells you how to separate the heading from the description in producing a complete catalogue entry.

You may either
- give the heading on a separate line above the description; or
- separate it from the description by a full stop and two spaces.

Optional rules   0.7

The rules recognize that libraries vary in the level of detail that they want in their catalogues, and so to some extent there are options within the rules to allow for this.

Some options should be matters of policy for a library. For example, you should decide whether you are going to use uniform titles or not, and for what kinds of material.

Keep a systematic record of your decisions about such matters, and follow your policy.

Other kinds of option can apply on a case by case basis, depending on the nature of the item.

The word 'prominently'   0.8

It might seem strange to provide a definition of a relatively common English word, but this is the most important rule in the whole chapter. In certain rules later on, we shall find the word 'prominently' used, and it is important to realize that in AACR2 it has a very specific meaning and is in a sense a 'technical term'.

If a rule says that a particular piece of information has to appear 'prominently' in the item being catalogued, this means that it must appear as a formal statement in one of the prescribed sources of information (see pp. 20–1) for areas 1 and 2, i.e. the Title and statement of responsibility area and the Publication, distribution, etc. area.

It is unfortunate that the areas of the description are never elsewhere referred to by numbers in this way (though it is perhaps implied by the paragraph numbering system), but this is what it means. If you don't understand this at the moment, don't worry. We shall see later that *where you take information from* is a very important aspect of cataloguing, and I hope that it will become clear as we go along. The main thing at this stage is to remember that this is where to look for the definition.

Judgement and interpretation   0.9

This section too is important, but in a different way. Beginning cataloguers usually expect that the rules of AACR2 will always provide an exact and uncontroversial answer to any cataloguing problem. Such, however, is not the case. The rules are deliberately framed in a general way, so as to show principles and to make them as widely applicable as possible. It is therefore inevitable that you will come across instances where you have to use your own judgement in how to apply a rule. Another cataloguer might come to a different solution to the problem, and in many cases the alternatives may be equally acceptable.

Cataloguing is *not* merely a mechanical process, consisting of the unthinking application of rules. It requires constant thinking and understanding. Some of the examples in this book have been chosen so as to illustrate the necessity for judgement.

Examples in AACR2

0.14

There are plenty of examples in AACR2, and I shall be giving you some more. The statement about the examples in AACR2 being illustrative rather than prescriptive is slightly puzzling. They should certainly be used as examples of how to do things, and I feel that you should be able to take them as authoritative.

Structure of a MARC record

The notes in the left-hand margin of this book give basic information about tags and subfields, and the Appendix gives MARC 21 records for all the specimen descriptions used in this book. The fields shown are only those with which AACR2 is concerned.

This book cannot provide a complete guide to the MARC format. For further information and background you are advised to consult books such as Byrne (1998). You should also consult the online manual available at the Library of Congress website (Library of Congress 2001), but *be careful*, because this includes certain fields and subfields that were designed for older cataloguing rules and are now redundant. In particular, use whatever documentation is provided for the system that you are using.

It is important to realize that it is AACR2 that gives you the rules to follow when producing catalogue records. MARC simply gives a structure to the records produced as a result of following the rules; MARC is not a cataloguing code in itself.

The basis of the MARC format is that the catalogue record is broken down into *fields*, which largely correspond to the *areas* of description in AACR2 but also include all the access points, together with certain information codes that are not covered by AACR2 at all.

A MARC record has three main parts:

- the record leader
- the directory
- the fields themselves.

As a cataloguer you will be mostly concerned with the third of these, but I will briefly explain what the first two are.

Record leader

This appears at the beginning of the record and contains coded data about the status of the record itself. It shows, for example, whether it is a new record or whether it has been edited. From a practical point of view you do not need to think about it, because all amendments are made automatically by the system itself.

Directory

This is a guide to the rest of the record, essentially a kind of index which shows where each of the other fields starts. You have to remember that the MARC format was developed in the days when electronic records could only be sent from place to place on magnetic tape. You cannot go instantly to a spot on a tape in the way you can with a disk, and the purpose of the directory is to ensure that the computer can find the required piece of information as efficiently as possible. The directory therefore lists the numeric tags for all the other fields, and shows their length and the position in the record where each one starts.

Again, you do not need to worry about this part of the record at all when you are cataloguing.

The fields themselves

Each field is introduced by a three-digit number called a *tag*, e.g. 008, 100, 245.

In most cases the field is broken down into *subfields*, using subfield codes. This makes a MARC record a bit hard to read when you first see one, but you soon get used to it when you are looking at them often.

In this book the MARC fields and subfields will be referred to in the left-hand margin when appropriate, to link them to the relevant sections of AACR2.

You will probably find that the appearance of subfields varies between different library systems. The subfield code consists of two characters:

- a 'delimiter', the character that introduces the subfield
- a lower-case letter, or occasionally a number.

In the Library of Congress online manual (Library of Congress 2001) the $ (dollar) sign is used as the delimiter, but some other systems use either the | (pipe) or ‡ (double dagger). This book will use the $ sign. In all cases the principle is the same.

Another difference you may notice is in the way in which subfields are displayed. Some systems start a new line for each subfield, while others run them on on the same line. In the catalogue record itself, as held in a computerized database, all the characters are run together anyway, so any difference is purely in the display, and is designed to make the record easier for cataloguers to read. You will obviously do whatever your system requires.

In some systems you will find that you have to put some kind of symbol at the *end* of a field, to ensure that whatever comes next is interpreted as being the tag for the next field. Some systems use # but others do not require anything, being set up so that the computer detects by other means where a field ends.

This brings us to one of the most important features of the MARC format, namely that (with a few exceptions) the fields can be of *variable length*. At the time of the development of MARC this was a very unusual feature in any database structure, but if you think about it you will realize that it is essential. Authors, titles and all the other parts of a catalogue record vary enormously in length, and it would be impossible to use a format which only allowed a certain number of characters in each field.

008 field

One of the first fields following the directory is the 008 field, which contains information in code form. The purpose of this is to assist retrieval; it is nothing to do with AACR2 cataloguing. It is of fixed length, and the codes go in fixed character positions. If input correctly this information can be invaluable in doing online searches, because it can allow you to search, for example, for children's works, or poetry, or biographies, or dictionaries. This kind of search would otherwise be very difficult to achieve.

Indicators

Each field starts with a three-digit *tag*. Following this, before the subfield codes start, there is usually room for up to two further digits, which are called *indicators*. It is not possible to generalize about these, because their purpose varies depending on the field where they occur. You can think of them as providing further definition of the tag, and you will see their uses as we go along.

The indicators are always of a *numeric* value, and either or both of them may be blank. In the marginal notes of this book a blank indicator value is shown by the underscore ('_').

List of the main MARC 21 fields

For convenience, I give here a list of the principal fields that you will see in a MARC 21 record. This is not a complete list, but is based on those that most closely refer to AACR2.

100	Main entry heading: personal author
110	Main entry heading: corporate body
111	Main entry heading: conference
130	Main entry heading: uniform title
240	Uniform title
243	Collective title
245	Title and statement of responsibility
250	Edition
260	Publication, etc.
300	Physical description
440	Series in added entry form
490	Series not in added entry form
5—	Notes
700	Added entry: person
710	Added entry: corporate body
711	Added entry: conference
8—	Added entry: series

You should immediately be able to see that there are some parallels between different tags, e.g. 100 and 700, 110 and 710. This should help you to remember them, and reduce the amount you have to learn. There is a similar correspondence in the subfields within those fields.

Punctuation

We shall see in the next chapter that AACR2 prescribes certain punctuation marks both between and within the areas (fields) in the catalogue record. Normally you will have to include the punctuation *within* a field together with the appropriate MARC 21 subfield codes. Punctuation *between* fields, or completely enclosing a field, such as Series statements being in parentheses, may or may not be supplied by the system.

4 Description

AACR2 Chapter 1 is designed to help you to describe *any* kind of material, including kinds that have not yet been invented. It is therefore written in rather general terms. To see how to deal with a specific physical form of material, look at Chapters 2–12, e.g. for printed books see AACR2 Chapter 2. But each of those chapters will keep referring you back to Chapter 1 for fuller information. You therefore really need to have a finger in Chapter 1 as you look at the rules in whichever chapter is relevant. Now that AACR2 has been issued in loose-leaf format it is easier to compare sections if you need to. To start with we shall stick to Chapter 1 as it gives the fullest information.

Areas of description   1.0B

In MARC these areas are known as *fields*.

The description is organized into a series of 'areas', as follows:

> Title and statement of responsibility
> Edition
> Material (or type of publication) specific details
> Publication, distribution, etc.
> Physical description
> Series
> Note
> Standard number and terms of availability

The order in which these areas appear cannot vary, and you will soon become familiar with this order. Not all of them are compulsory: several only appear when they are needed, and otherwise you can just ignore them. There is no need to show a blank space or anything like that; just miss them out. We shall see what is necessary as we go along.

Sources of information   1.0A1

The *most important thing* to get clear in your mind is that, whatever kind of material you are cataloguing, you are only allowed to take information from certain places in the item, and that *the places you are allowed use vary* depending on which area of the description you are dealing with. If you can remember this you are halfway to being a good cataloguer.

Each chapter of AACR2 starts with a list of the areas and the prescribed *sources of information*, as they are called, for that specific physical form of publication.

As an example, this means that, for the Title and statement of responsibility area of a book, you may take information *only* from the title page, whereas for the Edition area you have a greater range of sources.

2.0B

The important thing about all this is that *if* for any reason you need to include something that does *not* appear in the prescribed source for that area, you must enclose it in square brackets [...]. However, you should normally be very sparing about including anything of this kind at all.

1.0A1

Arrangement of the areas

1.0C

When you are writing a description according to AACR2, you have a choice of ways of showing where one area ends and the next begins. You can *either*

• start each area on a new line; *or*
• continue on the same line but separate each area from the previous one by the combination 'full stop space dash space' (. −).

If you are using MARC in a computerized system you may or may not find that the system will put the full stop in for you at the end of an area (field). You will have to do whatever is required in your system.

If you choose the latter, remember that the punctuation always *introduces* what follows, which means the *final* area does *not* end in a full stop.

This rule is rather hidden away in the first sentence of **1.0C**, and, as well as being based on ISBD, is a relic of the days of card catalogues. Most libraries then probably used to adopt a mixture of systems, e.g. running most of the areas on but perhaps starting the Note area on a new line. Nowadays most catalogues are OPACs, and very few OPACs provide for AACR2-style punctuation. You are therefore much more likely to see each area displayed starting on a new line, usually with a 'label' to show what it means. This is one of the areas in which AACR2 has rather lagged behind the reality of current cataloguing.

Punctuation

1.0C

It may seem strange to specify punctuation in such detail, and you might think it is unnecessary, but in fact this ties in with ISBD, which was mentioned in the Chapter 2, and is designed to help you distinguish between the different elements of the description.

Most of the rules about punctuation are the same as in real life.

For example, parentheses ( ) are closed up to the text that they enclose, i.e. you leave a space *outside* but not inside; commas are *followed* but not *preceded* by a space.

The two main exceptions are that:

MARC: You may be required to put a full stop even when nothing follows.

- punctuation always *precedes and introduces* something rather than concluding it (this means that a sentence only ends with a full stop if it is followed by something else)

  (because parentheses have to be in pairs, this does not quite apply to them)

- the colon and semicolon are always both *preceded* and followed by a space.

AACR2 Chapter 1 sets out the punctuation to be used *between* the areas of the description; the sections on individual areas give further details on the punctuation *within* each area. We shall look at these when we come to them.

Levels of description

AACR2 recognizes that not all libraries want the same amount of detail in catalogue entries, and therefore provides for three different 'levels' of description. These allow for certain elements of areas to be omitted.

As an example, look at the *first level*: if you follow this you can omit the *place of publication* of an item, while retaining the *publisher* and the *date*.

As uniformity increases with the spread of centrally produced records, it is likely that fewer libraries will create catalogue records to the first level only, but of course each library can always specify which parts of a more detailed record it actually wishes to use and display.

You will find that most of the national libraries and cataloguing cooperatives specify that records should confirm to at least the *second level*. This includes nearly all the possible elements, and differs very little from the full *third level*.

Copying

Before we go any further, a word about copying. Much of cataloguing consists of copying. Copying what is in front of you is the easiest and the hardest thing in the world. It is here that you can so easily make mistakes, so do be very careful. Be especially careful with words that have alternative spellings, like 'organization', because it is your job to copy the spelling that appears in the source of information. You might think it would be more helpful to standardize spellings, and of course it would, but you are not allowed to do so. And remember that 'fore-word' is not 'forward'.

As we go on, you will see that the extent to which you have to copy keeps changing as we move from area to area in the description.

Errors in the original   1.0F

This rule appears early on because it can apply to all kinds of errors, in different areas of the description. We shall look at a specific example of a title in due course (Fig. 4.10). If you see something which is obviously wrong, you can either

- supply the correction in square brackets; or
- indicate that you have seen the mistake (and that it is not yours!) by adding '[sic]'.

The important thing is that *you must copy the error as you find it* because it is part of your job to copy what is in front of you.

Exactly what you do to indicate the error will depend on what kind of mistake it is. Anyone can tell that 'wolrd' ought to read 'world', but it is not obvious that 'Buck' ought to be 'Brick'; hence the differing treatments.

But think of the users of the catalogue. How will they find the item if they don't know that there is a mistake? Many OPACs work on a keyword basis; users who look for a word that is not there because it is misprinted will not find the item. You should therefore usually make an added entry under the corrected form. But this is taking us to access points, which are a different part of the cataloguing process.

Some items have fictitious publication details. If you know this, make the   1.4B6
appropriate corrections in square brackets after copying what appears in the item.

Sometimes the date of publication of an item may be wrong. Here again it   1.4F2
will be more sensible to add the correct date in square brackets, but you must still copy the wrong date first.

MARC:
245 field

Title and statement of responsibility area   1.1

This is the most important area of the description and is naturally given first. It is the one compulsory area, because without it you have nothing at all to identify the item, and so it *must* exist in every catalogue record.

Sources of information

For books, the chief source of information for this area is the title page;   2.0B1
this means the title page itself, not the back of it. However, you *are* allowed to use a combination of facing pages (e.g. Fig. 4.6, Fig. 10.1)

or even successive leaves if they give the required information without repetition.

There are other sources that can be used in certain special circumstances, and you should read the full rule for these.

With commercially published books and other published items, there is seldom any problem about finding the information you need on the title page. With less mainstream publications, however, such as research reports or 'grey literature', you will often find that there is no title page as such, but only a cover.

What should you do in these cases? My view is that you should treat the cover as the chief source of information and use the information presented on it without square brackets, adding a Note area to explain that the title is from the cover, e.g.

> Cover title   **2.7B4**

or

> Title from cover

This may not strictly be correct, but it seems to me to be justified by the wording of the rule. It is not as if you were making up something that does not appear on the publication at all, and in these cases the cover really *is* the title page.

2.0B1

The elements of this area

The Title and statement of responsibility area may include several elements:

MARC:
245

$a

$h

$b

$b

$c

Note: $b can be used only once; it can therefore be used for *either* other title information *or* parallel title.

- title proper
- general material designation
- parallel title(s)
- other title information
- statement(s) of responsibility

We shall go through these in turn.

They may not appear in this order in the chief source of information. If they do not, you are allowed to transpose them, *provided that they are not grammatically linked together.*

1.1A2

For example, it is quite common for the author's name to be at the top of the title page but the title itself further down (see Fig. 5.11, p. 111). In this case you would copy the title itself first.

Any elements that are linked have to be kept in the order in which they appear.

In each of them you are copying out details from the chief source of information; in the case of a book, this will be the title page.

2.0B2

Sources of information for non-book materials

Sound recordings 6.0B1

There is a list of different sources depending on the physical form of the recording, but notice that generally you should prefer *textual* to *sound* data.

This means that if you are dealing with the recording of a radio programme, you should make sure that you label it in such a way as to give you the details you need.

Videos 7.0B1

In contrast to sound recordings, here you prefer information from within the item itself, and there is an order of preference:

- the item itself (i.e. the title frames)
- its container.

If neither of these is available you can take information from accompanying material, the container, or other sources.

Most videos do have a title within the item, and the only problem arises if you have not got facilities for viewing videos where you are doing the cataloguing.

Electronic resources 9.0B1

Here again you have to prefer information from within the resource itself. This means that if you are cataloguing a web page you will look at the initial display of the page itself. If you are dealing with a computer disk you will play it and see what comes up as the title.

Only if these fail do you go on to look at other information, such as metadata, or, in the case of a disk, the label on the disk.

MARC:
245 $a

Title proper 1.1B

Title proper is the formal name used in AACR2 for the main title, or what most people would just refer to as the *title* of an item. Everything you catalogue has to have one. This means that if there isn't one you are allowed to make one up, putting it in square brackets, and this is particularly necessary if you are cataloguing an object of some kind.

Exceptions to copying 1.1B1

I have said that you are basically copying, and this applies throughout

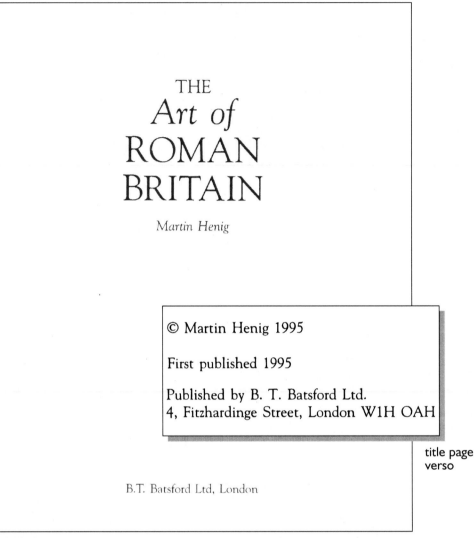

THE
Art of
ROMAN
BRITAIN

Martin Henig

© Martin Henig 1995

First published 1995

Published by B. T. Batsford Ltd.
4, Fitzhardinge Street, London W1H OAH

title page
verso

B.T. Batsford Ltd, London

Fig. 4.1

the Title and statement of responsibility area. But there are some exceptions, and we immediately see one of them. You do *not* necessarily copy

- punctuation
- capitalization.

This is because *punctuation* is 'imposed' by AACR2. Often it is convenient, and best, to copy the punctuation that appears in the chief source, but it is not essential to do so. If AACR2 requires a particular form of punctuation (e.g. to separate elements of an area) you will insert it even though it is not there in the actual item.

As for *capitalization*, the best thing is just to try to imagine that you are writing an ordinary sentence in the language of the title, i.e. start with a capital letter but don't use any others except for words that have to have them in all circumstances. Put out of your mind the fact that it is a title at all.　　**A.4**

Many people find this hard to begin with, but you must fight against the Natural Tendency to Endow all Titles with Plenty of Capital Letters. Obviously words like Wednesday will continue to get them.

If it weren't for this rule, we should have to copy the capitalization as we found it, and this would produce some very peculiar and inconsistent catalogue descriptions. After all, MANY BOOKS HAVE TITLES IN SOLID CAPITALS, and it would look strange if we copied those out when they occurred.

Example
(Fig. 4.1, opposite) We put, not

✘ THE *Art of* ROMAN BRITAIN

but

✓ The art of Roman Britain

Beware of different capitalization systems in different languages, and always consult **Appendix A** until you get used to it.　　**App. A**

It is fairly well known, for example, that German uses capitals for all nouns. Conversely, adjectives of nationality, like 'British', 'French', etc., which are always capitalized in English, are almost invariably lower case in other languages.　　**A.40A1**　**A.39A1,**　**A.40B1,**　**etc.**

Remember too that (in English) the name of any corporate body will get Capital Letters for the Principal Words; this includes named conferences. This means that before you can copy the title correctly you need to have made the decision as to whether the conference has a name (see p. 92).

Incidentally, there is no provision in AACR2 for copying features like *italic*, **bold** or underlining when transcribing information. You just have to put it all in ordinary roman.

Sometimes the typographic arrangement of the title page gives great prominence to a particular word in the title. Provided that the whole title is connected together, you have to ignore this and copy it as it stands.

The Natural History of

MOLES

Martyn L. Gorman and R. David Stone

© 1990 Martyn L. Gorman and R. David Stone
Christopher Helm (Publishers) Ltd, Imperial House,
21–25 North Street, Bromley, Kent BR1 1SD

Line illustrations by Robert Donaldson and Bob Duthie

ISBN 0–7470–1214–8

title page verso

Christopher Helm Mammal Series
Edited by Dr Ernest Neal, MBE, former President of the Mammal Society

page opposite title page

CHRISTOPHER HELM
London

Fig. 4.2

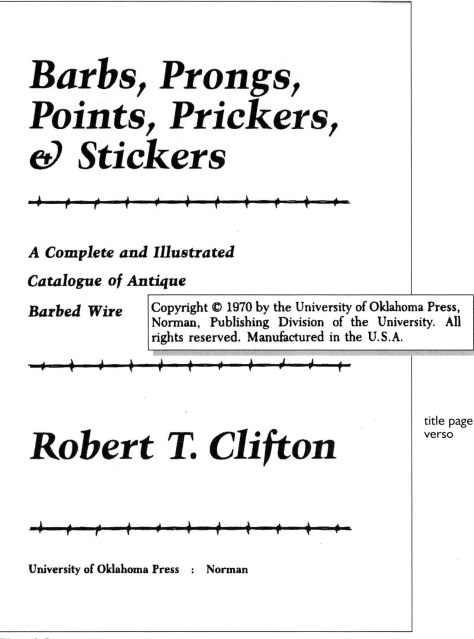

Fig. 4.3

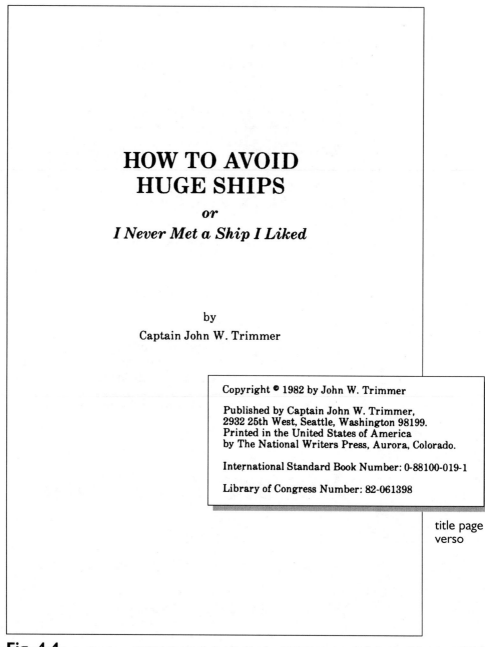

HOW TO AVOID
HUGE SHIPS

or
I Never Met a Ship I Liked

by
Captain John W. Trimmer

Copyright © 1982 by John W. Trimmer

Published by Captain John W. Trimmer,
2932 25th West, Seattle, Washington 98199.
Printed in the United States of America
by The National Writers Press, Aurora, Colorado.

International Standard Book Number: 0-88100-019-1

Library of Congress Number: 82-061398

title page
verso

Fig. 4.4

Example

(Fig. 4.2, p. 28)

```
The natural history of moles
```

Because you are copying, you must copy an ampersand ('&') as it appears, and not replace it with the word 'and'.

Example

(Fig. 4.3, p. 29)

```
Barbs, prongs, points, prickers & stickers
```

Notice here that I have omitted the comma after 'prickers', because this is the slightly commoner British practice, and we are *not* copying punctuation.

MARC: no special coding

Alternative titles

1.1B1

An alternative title is always introduced by 'or' or its equivalent, and you should put a comma both before and after it. The whole thing is part of the title proper, and should be included as such. Don't treat it like 'other title information' (see below, pp. 36–40). The alternative title is like a fresh title, which is why it gets a capital letter of its own. You will seldom see any modern publications with an alternative title, but they were fashionable at one time.

Example

(Fig. 4.4, opposite)

```
How to avoid huge ships, or, I never met a ship I
liked
```

Punctuation marks

1.1B1

If you see '...' in the title you do not copy these dots: you replace them with a long dash. This is because dots are what *you* use in certain cases if you need to show that you have missed something out (see pp. 40, 49–50).

Similarly, if the title contains square brackets, you have to replace them with round, because square brackets would be used for *your* (rare) additions.

1.1B1

Example

(Fig. 4.5, overleaf)

Not

```
✘ Why does my rabbit … ?
```

but

```
✔ Why does my rabbit - ?
```

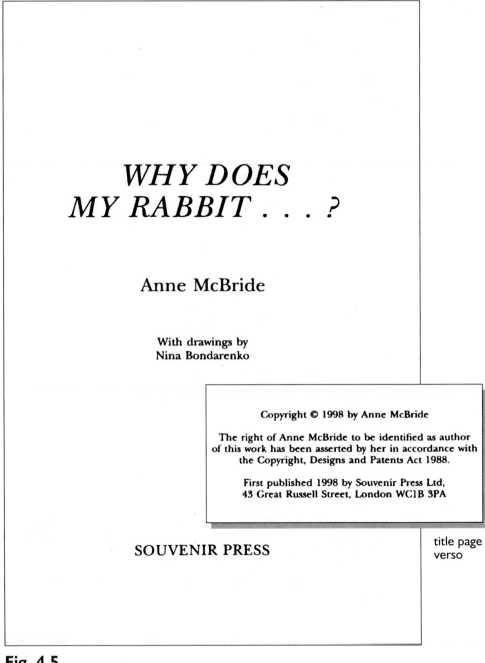

WHY DOES MY RABBIT . . . ?

Anne McBride

With drawings by
Nina Bondarenko

SOUVENIR PRESS

title page
verso

Fig. 4.5

Statements of responsibility as part of title

1.1B2

Sometimes the title includes a statement of responsibility *grammatically connected* to it. In this case you cannot remove it and separate it from the title proper; you must include it. This is particularly common with inflected languages like Latin.

Again it is advisable to make an *added entry* for the 'title' part of the title, e.g.

> More beautiful you in twenty-one days

because otherwise someone looking for that title is unlikely to find it.

Because of the way MARC 21 works you will have to omit the initial 'A' in making the added entry: 246 field

---

Example
(Fig. 10.4, p. 195)

> John Betjeman's collected poems

There is some similarity between the cases covered by this rule and those covered by the new rule introduced in the 2002 revision of AACR2, and it is unfortunate that they lead to opposite results. If the title proper starts with introductory words that are 'not intended to be part of the title' you may omit them, and give the complete title including them in a Note area.

1.1B1

1.7B4

Although there is much sense in this, a good case could be made for applying this rule to *Eileen Ford's a more beautiful you in twenty-one days* because surely the words 'Eileen Ford's' would equally be understood by most normal people as not being part of the actual title. On the other hand, doing so would make titles such as *Homeri opera* harder to deal with. As a rule of thumb you will just have to assume that the Eileen Ford rule applies only to names in the possessive case. Use your discretion in applying the other rule.

Titles consisting solely of a person's name

1.1B3

Sometimes the title consists merely of the name of the person responsible for the item; this is especially common with art catalogues and with complete texts of classical authors. In this case you simply copy out the name as the title proper and leave it at that.

General material designation

1.1C

The general material designation is an *optional* addition. It was first included in ISBD as a means of showing the physical form of an item in an obvious place in the description, rather than relying on the Physical description area, which catalogue users might easily miss. It therefore comes here, *immediately following the title proper*, and before any other part of this area.

MARC: 245 $h

It is a different kind of element, because it is something which you do *not* copy from the chief source of information, but which you take from a list of authorized terms. This of course is also why it must appear in square brackets. It is thus a kind of interlude in the copying process.

For printed books it is normal to omit this element altogether: I do not know of any library that includes it.

But for other physical formats it is useful to include it, because it immediately alerts users to the format. In the UK use the terms in List 1 and in the USA those in List 2. (This is one of the very few places in which AACR2 is not really a united code.) The lists are rather a strange mixture, and do not provide adequately for electronic materials. An electronic text, for example, would be described as 'electronic resource' rather than 'text', which would presumably only apply to printed books.

1.1C1

You will therefore put things like

```
Antony Gormley [videorecording]

Hancock's half hour [sound recording]

The ladykillers [videorecording]

Life on earth [videorecording]

Overcrowded, under-utilised or just right?
[electronic resource]
```

Keep a record of your policy as to when and when not to use it.

Notice that the word used goes in square brackets and starts with a small letter. In other words, it is just a sort of attachment to the title proper, and not the start of a fresh sentence.

MARC:
245 $b if it has
not already been
used

Parallel titles

1.1D

We now come back to our transcription of the chief source of information.

Sometimes an item has its title in more than one language. In this case (unless you are using only first level description) you copy out both (or all) languages. Use the equals sign preceded and followed by a space (=) to separate the languages; this is easy to remember, because the titles are *equivalents*. Also, because they are regarded as equals, the parallel title starts again with a capital letter just like the title proper.

Note that *both (or all) the titles must appear on the chief source of information at the same time.* You do *not* use this system for works which are translations where only one language appears. Beginners often confuse it with a *uniform title*, which is something quite different (see pp. 184–5). The commonest occurrences are

- parallel texts, where the item has both languages side by side right through
- proceedings of international conferences, where chapters may be written in different languages and there is often a multi-lingual title page.

There are special rules about how to deal with parallel titles in Other title information and Statements of responsibility.

1.1E5
1.1F10

Fig. 4.6

Example
(Fig. 4.6, above)

```
Latin for all occasions = Lingua Latina
occasionibus omnibus
```

Note that we shall have to make an adjustment to this when we come to statements of responsibility (see below, pp. 52–3).

    The double-page spread of title page and facing page have been taken together as forming the chief source of information. I have put the English title first because conventionally we expect the title page to be on the right; I therefore regard the left-hand page as subordinate. But if the information had been spread right across the double page it could all have been taken together. **2.0B1**

    'Latina' has been capitalized in accordance with the rules; in most languages such a word would not be capitalized. **A.43A, A.14A**

MARC:
245 $b which is
not repeatable;
for subsequent
occurrences use
punctuation only.

Other title information

1.1E

This is the type of information which we usually think of as a *subtitle*, i.e. an explanation or elaboration of the title proper. It is not the same thing as a part-title, which divides a work into, say, two or more volumes. It is preceded by 'space colon space' (:).

Example

(Fig. 4.3, p. 29)

```
Barbs, prongs, points, prickers & stickers :
a complete and illustrated catalogue of
antique barbed wire
```

(Fig. 4.7, opposite)

```
Riches of the wild : land mammals of South-
East Asia
```

(Notice here that we give 'south-east' capital letters because 'South-East Asia' is the name of a region. Ordinarily words like 'south' would *not* have capitals.)

A.15A1

(Fig. 4.8, p. 38)

```
Rabbit hutches on postage stamps : economics,
planning and development in the 1990s
```

Note that in the last example the colon which happened already to be at the end of the title proper is replaced with AACR2's standard 'space colon space'.

It is possible to have two or more pieces of other title information, in which case you transcribe them all, giving the same punctuation at the start of each.

You can usually tell where the other title information starts from the layout of the chief source of information. Sometimes it may actually *precede* the title proper but be obviously other title information, and in this case, as I have mentioned, you are allowed to transpose the two elements.

1.1A2

Occasionally it is hard to tell whether some words are other title information or part of the title proper. In this case it is a good guide to look at other places in the item where the title appears (e.g. for a book: on the spine, the cover, in running titles) and see whether the words appear there or not. If they never do, it is a safe bet that you can treat them as other title information.

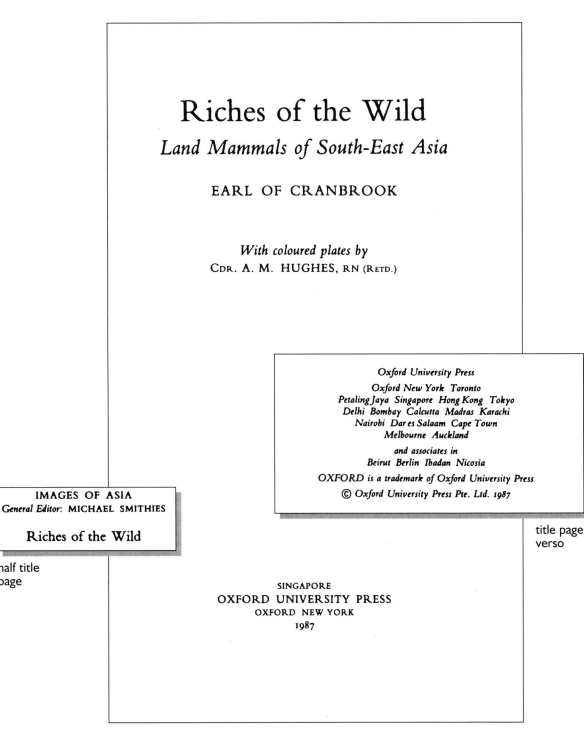

Riches of the Wild
Land Mammals of South-East Asia

EARL OF CRANBROOK

With coloured plates by
CDR. A. M. HUGHES, RN (RETD.)

IMAGES OF ASIA
General Editor: MICHAEL SMITHIES

Riches of the Wild

half title
page

Oxford University Press

Oxford New York Toronto
Petaling Jaya Singapore Hong Kong Tokyo
Delhi Bombay Calcutta Madras Karachi
Nairobi Dar es Salaam Cape Town
Melbourne Auckland

and associates in
Beirut Berlin Ibadan Nicosia

OXFORD is a trademark of Oxford University Press

© *Oxford University Press Pte. Ltd. 1987*

title page
verso

SINGAPORE
OXFORD UNIVERSITY PRESS
OXFORD NEW YORK
1987

Fig. 4.7

The 12th Denman Lecture, 1990

Rabbit hutches on postage stamps: Economics, planning and development in the 1990s

Alan Evans

University of Cambridge, Department of Land Economy
19 Silver Street, Cambridge CB3 9EP

Published by Granta Editions Limited, a wholly owned imprint of Book Production Consultants.

© Alan Evans, 1990

title page verso

GRANTA EDITIONS

Fig. 4.8

DOGS
THAT KNOW
WHEN THEIR
OWNERS ARE
COMING HOME

*and other unexplained
powers of animals*

Rupert Sheldrake

Copyright © Rupert Sheldrake 1999

First published in the United Kingdom in 1999
by Hutchinson

Random House UK Limited
20 Vauxhall Bridge Road, London SW1V 2SA

Random House Australia (Pty) Limited
20 Alfred Street, Milsons Point, Sydney
New South Wales 2061, Australia

Random House New Zealand Limited
18 Poland Road, Glenfield,
Auckland 10, New Zealand

Random House South Africa (Pty) Limited
Endulini, 5A Jubilee Road, Parktown 2193,
South Africa

HUTCHINSON
London

title page
verso

Fig. 4.9

Examples

(Fig. 4.9, p. 39)

This is a good example of this problem. I should be inclined to put

```
Dogs that know when their owners are coming home :
and other unexplained powers of animals
```

that is, treating 'and other unexplained powers of animals' as Other title information, because otherwise it makes the title proper unduly long. On the spine the title stops at that point. If the title proper were very short it might be treated differently.

(Fig. 5.9, p. 101)

```
Pre-Raphaelite drawings in the British Museum
```

In this case it makes more sense to put the whole thing in as the title proper despite the layout of the title page.

1.1E3

You can shorten 'lengthy other title information', i.e. long subtitles. You will seldom need to do this for modern books, but for older material it can be useful as older books sometimes have very long subtitles.

Example

(Fig. 10.2, p. 188)

```
The life and strange surprizing adventures of
Robinson Crusoe, of York, mariner : who lived
eight and twenty years …
```

1.1E4

Statements of responsibility may be included in other title information just as they may be in title proper, and similar provisions apply.

Statements of responsibility

1.1F

What is a statement of responsibility? What has it got to do with titles? These are questions that often puzzle beginners.

'Statement of responsibility' is a general way of describing words that usually appear in the chief source of information to show who has written, composed, edited, illustrated or in other ways contributed to the existence of the item.

For books we usually mean authors, editors, illustrators, writers of forewords; for other items the nature of responsibility will be different but the principle remains the same. The word 'responsibility' is used because it is broad enough to include all possibilities.

On videos you may find a statement about the presenter or performer, or the writer. On sound recordings the performer is likely to be mentioned.

Why should it be included here when on the face of it it is quite separate from the title? The simple answer is 'because it is there in the chief source of information'. You might expect this kind of information to be dealt with in the access points, and of course it is, but you need to remember that AACR2 completely separates the process of description from that of assigning access points. At this stage, therefore, you are just copying what is there, and not thinking at all about which (if any) of these names is going to get an access point, or about the form of name which you might use for that access point.

MARC:
245 $c, which is
not repeatable:
use just
punctuation for
subsequent
statements

The first statement of responsibility is preceded by 'space slash space' (/).   **1.1A1**

In most cases you just copy out what is in front of you.

Examples

(Fig. 4.1, p. 26)

```
The art of Roman Britain / Martin Henig
```

(Fig. 4.2, p. 28)

```
The natural history of moles / Martyn L.
Gorman and R. David Stone
```

(Fig. 4.3, p. 29)

```
Barbs, prongs, points, prickers & stickers :
a complete and illustrated catalogue of
antique barbed wire / Robert T. Clifton
```

(Fig. 4.7, p. 37)

```
Riches of the wild : land mammals of South-
East Asia / Earl of Cranbrook
```

(Fig. 4.8, p. 38)

```
Rabbit hutches on postage stamps : economics,
planning and development in the 1990s / Alan
Evans
```

(Fig. 4.10, overleaf)

```
Melchanolies [sic] of knowledge : literature
in the age of science / edited by Margery
Arent Safir
```

Note the insertion of '[sic]' here to indicate the error.   **1.0F1**

You can include more than one statement of responsibility but each after

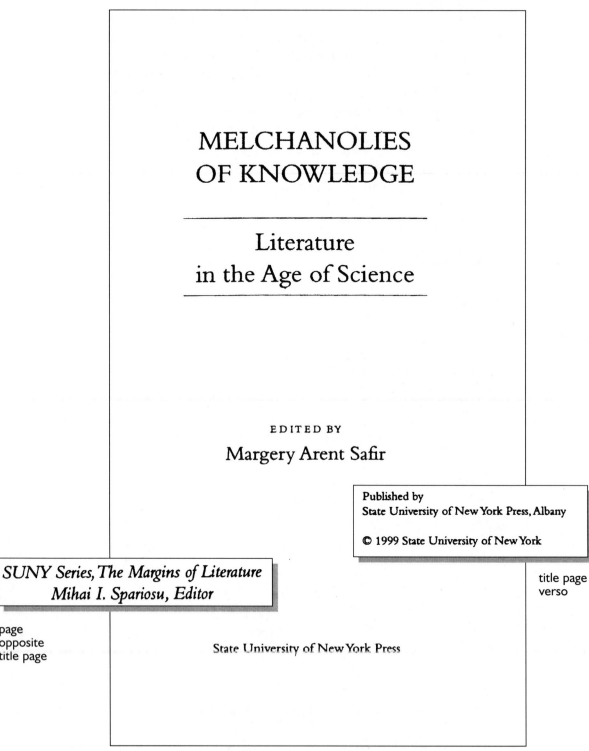

MELCHANOLIES
OF KNOWLEDGE

Literature
in the Age of Science

EDITED BY
Margery Arent Safir

Published by
State University of New York Press, Albany

© 1999 State University of New York

SUNY Series, The Margins of Literature
Mihai I. Spariosu, Editor

title page
verso

page
opposite
title page

State University of New York Press

Fig. 4.10

VOLUME FOUR OF A HISTORY OF CHESHIRE
GENERAL EDITOR—J. J. BAGLEY

CHESHIRE UNDER THE
NORMAN EARLS
1066 – 1237

by

B. M. C. HUSAIN

CARTOGRAPHY BY A. G. HODGKISS

First published 1973

© B. M. C. Husain

title page verso

PUBLISHED BY THE CHESHIRE COMMUNITY COUNCIL
PUBLICATIONS TRUST LIMITED
WATERGATE HOUSE
WATERGATE STREET
CHESTER

Fig. 4.11

the first is preceded by 'space semicolon space' (;).   **1.1A1**

This is probably the only place in AACR2 where repetition of an element uses a different form of punctuation from that for the first occurrence.

Examples
(Fig. 4.5, p. 32)

```
Why does my rabbit - ? / Anne McBride ; with
drawings by Nina Bondarenko
```

(Fig. 4.11, p. 43)

```
Cheshire under the Norman earls : 1066-1237 /
by B.M.C. Husain ; cartography by A.G.
Hodgkiss
```

(Notice the full stops and spacing in the last example. In statements of responsibility AACR2 requires full stop and *no space between* initials,   **1.1B6** but then full stop *and* space *after* the final initial.

If no full stops appear, you should insert them as a matter of uniformity, because you are *not* copying punctuation.)

Occasionally you need to *add something*.

If there is no statement of responsibility at all, it will often be all right simply not to put anything. But sometimes the author's name may appear somewhere else in the item, and not in the chief source. If it appears in one of the places that counts as 'prominently' you are   **0.8** allowed to add it yourself in square brackets, as in the third example   **1.1F1** under **1.1F1**.

This is one example of the importance of remembering the definition of   **0.8** 'prominently'.

The usual occasion for adding statements like this is when a statement appears on the back of the title page of a book rather than on the title page itself.

Examples
(Fig. 4.12, opposite)

```
All I need to know in life I learned from romance
novels / [Victoria M. Johnson]
```

In this case the name of the author appears only in the copyright statement on the back of the title page, and on the cover.

All I Need to
Know in Life
I Learned
From
Romance
Novels

title page
verso

Fig. 4.12

(Fig. 8.1, p. 156)

```
Advances in artificial intelligence : 12th
Biennial Conference of the Canadian Society for
Computational Studies of Intelligence, AI'98,
Vancouver, BC, Canada, June 18-20, 1998 :
proceedings / [editors Robert E. Mercer, Eric
Neufeld]
```

Here again the names of the editors appear only the back of the title page. They may form a useful access point, and so should be included in a statement of responsibility.

You should *not* use this as an excuse to construct lengthy statements that do not exist in the item; if the name does not appear 'prominently' you cannot add it, and such things, if really necessary, are best left to the Note area (see pp. 81–3).

1.1F2

Points to note about copying statements of responsibility:

- if the word 'by' appears, include it
- if the word 'by' does not appear, do not include it.

This may seem obvious, because it follows from the general rule about copying, but at one time it was common to add '[by]' when it did not appear; this is now quite out of fashion.

The same applies to 'and' connecting two or more names: if it appears, you copy it out. But what happens if it does not appear? Here there is a problem. If there are two names, and no 'and', how are catalogue users to know where one name ends and the next begins? The usual thing is to use a comma (followed by a space) to separate them. Because you are not necessarily copying punctuation you are allowed to do this.

If the statement of responsibility appears *before* the title proper you can transpose it to its correct AACR2 position, provided that it is not grammatically linked to the title proper. If it is grammatically linked, you have to leave it where it is.

1.1F3

Example
(Fig. 5.11, p. 111)

```
Great expectations / Charles Dickens ; retold by
Florence Bell
```

Sometimes beginners are puzzled about what counts as a separate statement: do two authors amount to two statements of responsibility?

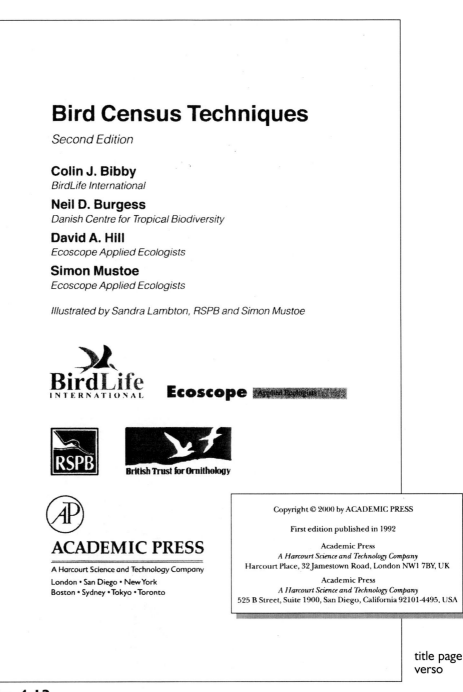

Bird Census Techniques

Second Edition

Colin J. Bibby
BirdLife International

Neil D. Burgess
Danish Centre for Tropical Biodiversity

David A. Hill
Ecoscope Applied Ecologists

Simon Mustoe
Ecoscope Applied Ecologists

Illustrated by Sandra Lambton, RSPB and Simon Mustoe

BirdLife
INTERNATIONAL

Ecoscope Applied Ecologists

RSPB

British Trust for Ornithology

ACADEMIC PRESS

A Harcourt Science and Technology Company
London • San Diego • New York
Boston • Sydney • Tokyo • Toronto

Copyright © 2000 by ACADEMIC PRESS

First edition published in 1992

Academic Press
A Harcourt Science and Technology Company
Harcourt Place, 32 Jamestown Road, London NW1 7BY, UK

Academic Press
A Harcourt Science and Technology Company
525 B Street, Suite 1900, San Diego, California 92101-4495, USA

title page
verso

Fig. 4.13

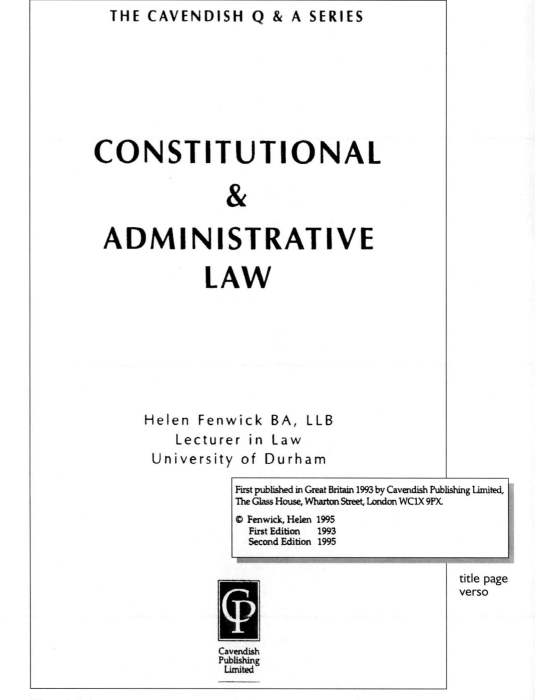

THE CAVENDISH Q & A SERIES

CONSTITUTIONAL
&
ADMINISTRATIVE
LAW

Helen Fenwick BA, LLB
Lecturer in Law
University of Durham

First published in Great Britain 1993 by Cavendish Publishing Limited,
The Glass House, Wharton Street, London WC1X 9PX.

© Fenwick, Helen 1995
  First Edition   1993
  Second Edition 1995

title page
verso

Cavendish
Publishing
Limited

Fig. 4.14

The answer is No: generally speaking, each *different kind* of responsibility needs a separate statement.

Sometimes you will see a statement of responsibility that clearly indicates different *kinds* of responsibility but where the names are linked with 'and' or some other connecting word. In this case you take it as a single statement.

So if an item has two authors followed by two editors followed by two illustrators it will need three statements of responsibility:

- one for the two authors
- a second for the two editors
- a third for the two illustrators.

Doubts about what is a statement of responsibility

Sometimes you may be uncertain as to whether a piece of information counts as statement of responsibility or not. Some rules help you with this:

If a noun phrase occurs in conjunction with a statement of responsibility treat it as other title information if it indicates the nature of the work.   **1.1F12**

But if it indicates the role of the person concerned, treat it as part of the statement of responsibility.

Sometimes a statement of responsibility does not include any named person or organization; it can still count as a statement of responsibility.   **1.1F14**

A statement of responsibility may include words which are neither names nor linking words.

You should omit anything that does not constitute either other title information or a statement of responsibility. The commonest occurrence of this is   **1.1F15**
information about the number or type of illustrations, which, unless it includes someone's name, should be removed to the Physical description area.

Example
(Fig. 5.14, p. 118)
```
        Howard Hodgkin / Andrew Graham-Dixon
```

More exceptions to copying

We now come to an important rule which provides another *exception to copying*.

In each statement of responsibility you can transcribe only up to *three*   **1.1F5**
names; if there are more than three, you copy the *first only* and follow it with ' ... [et al.]' (meaning 'and others': don't forget the full stop after the 'al'). The three dots with the space both before and after them constitute the 'mark of omission' and show that you have missed something

out. Don't be tempted to take pity on the other named persons; you are forbidden to mention them in any way.

There is a lesson for us all here: if you write a book in collaboration with other people, and you want to be mentioned in the catalogue, either don't collaborate with more then two people or make sure your name appears first on the title page.

Note that this rule applies to each statement of responsibility separately: in the unlikely event of an item's having three authors followed by three editors followed by three illustrators followed by three writers of prefaces, because each group of three names would form a separate statement you would be allowed to copy out all twelve names.

Examples
(Fig. 4.13, p. 47)

```
Bird census techniques / Colin J. Bibby … [et
al.] ; illustrated by Sandra Lambton, RSPB
and Simon Mustoe
```

We cannot mention Burgess, Hill or Mustoe as authors. But we start again with the second statement of responsibility, relating to the illustrators, which means that Mustoe gets a mention there.

There are still more exceptions to copying. You must miss out various titles and forms of address which sometimes precede names, and also letters and descriptions after names. This is a very useful rule because it allows you to omit lists of letters, or job titles, that some people put after their names.

1.1F7

Examples
(Fig. 4.4, p. 30)

```
How to avoid huge ships, or, I never met a
ship I liked / by John W. Trimmer
```

not

```
✗ / by Captain John W. Trimmer
```

(Fig. 4.14, p. 48)

```
Constitutional & administrative law / Helen
Fenwick
```

not

```
✗  / Helen Fenwick BA, LLB, Lecturer in Law,
   University of Durham
```

(Fig. 4.7, p. 37)

```
Riches of the wild : land mammals of South-
East Asia / Earl of Cranbrook ; with coloured
plates by A.M. Hughes
```

not

```
✗ ; with coloured plates by Cdr. A.M. Hughes,
  RN (retd.)
```

Note too that we cannot abbreviate 'coloured' in this area of the **B.4A**
description, though we can in the Physical description area.

If the book simply said 'with coloured plates' we would ignore this
statement altogether.

In Fig. 5.4 (p. 93) we can ignore all the material which appears at the
top of the title page, and could still do so if it were placed next to the
statement of responsibility.

Notice especially

- the British terms of honour at (d) are *only* the four mentioned, no **1.1F7d**
  others
- in each of these cases when you omit something you do *not* use the
  three dots (mark of omission).

The odd thing here really is the appearance of 'the late' in the final example.
There is nothing very specific in the opening sentence of the rule, and one
can only assume that it is implied by the 'etc.' there. Fortunately occurrences
of any other words are very rare, but under this rule they should probably
be omitted.

Adding to statements of responsibility **1.1F8**

You can *add* a 'short word or phrase' if necessary. You should be very,
very sparing in using this rule, and apply it only in cases where leaving the statement as it is would be grossly misleading, e.g. when
someone appears to have written the book but has in fact only edited
it. In this case you could add

```
[edited by]
```

to make the situation clear.

I have already mentioned that you would *not* use it to add words
like 'by' or 'and'. And do not use it as an excuse to add all kinds of

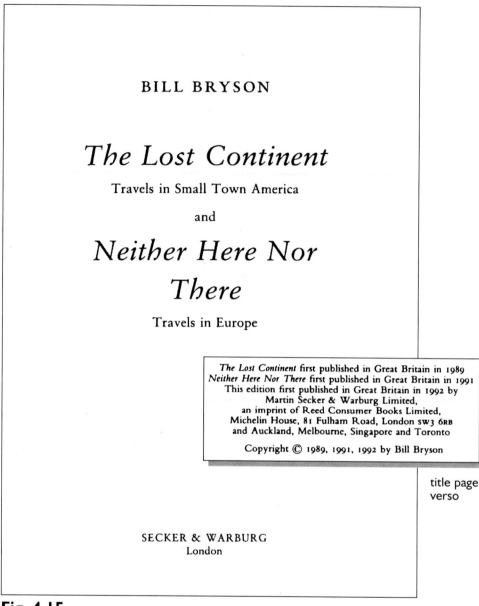

BILL BRYSON

The Lost Continent

Travels in Small Town America

and

Neither Here Nor There

Travels in Europe

The Lost Continent first published in Great Britain in 1989
Neither Here Nor There first published in Great Britain in 1991
This edition first published in Great Britain in 1992 by
Martin Secker & Warburg Limited,
an imprint of Reed Consumer Books Limited,
Michelin House, 81 Fulham Road, London SW3 6RB
and Auckland, Melbourne, Singapore and Toronto

Copyright © 1989, 1991, 1992 by Bill Bryson

title page
verso

SECKER & WARBURG
London

Fig. 4.15

miscellaneous information, however useful you may feel it would be
to the user.

Parallel titles and statements of responsibility

1.1F10

If an item has a parallel title and also parallel statements of responsibility, you
copy out each language at a time. We therefore now have to adjust our previous example:

Example

(Fig. 4.6, p. 35)

```
Latin for all occasions / by Henry Beard = Lingua
Latina occasionibus omnibus / Henricus Barbatus
scripsit
```

Sometimes an item has its title in more than one language but the statement of responsibility in only one language, or vice versa, and these rules tell you what to do here.

1.1F10
1.1F11

Items without a collective title

1.1G

An item that has no 'collective title' is one which physically contains more than one individual work but does not have an overall title for the whole thing. It is comparatively rare in modern books, and I will not go into all the details here, but this is an example:

Example

(Fig. 4.15, opposite)

```
The lost continent : travels in small town America
; and, Neither here nor there : travels in Europe
/ Bill Bryson
```

> ## Summary of Title and statement of responsibility area
>
> Copy what is in front of you *except*
>
> - capitalization
> - punctuation
> - order of elements, *unless they are grammatically linked*
> - if more than three names in statement of responsibility, omit all after first
> - omit certain terms of address and descriptions attached to names.

MARC:
250

Edition area

1.2

In moving into this area we find two differences:

- the sources of information that you can use are different, and (for most formats) you have more flexibility
- what you put down is not such an *exact* copy as it was in the Title and statement of responsibility area.

You base what you write in the Edition area on what appears in the item, but now you are allowed to – indeed *must* – abbreviate certain words according to the instructions, i.e. change numerals to their numeric,

1.2B,
B.5A1

ordinal, form and abbreviate certain words meaning 'edition', etc.

Example
(Fig. 4.14, p. 48)
Although the book says 'Second Edition' we put:

```
Constitutional & administrative law / Helen
Fenwick. - 2nd ed.
```

Notice also that in this case the edition statement is on the *back* of the title page; this is perfectly acceptable in this area of the description, whereas it would not be acceptable in the Title and statement of responsibility area.

Note the silliness of **1.2B2**. Personally I would ignore this and put   **1.2B2**

```
[3rd] ed.
```

as this is clearly what 'Three asterisks' is supposed to mean.

When you look at **Appendix C** for numerals you will find that usage   **App. C**
varies considerably according to the language concerned. So don't
assume that you know what the abbreviation should be: *check*.

Notice too that the English abbreviations are '1st', '2nd', '3rd', etc.,   **C.8A**
not '1st', '2nd', '3rd', whereas in some other languages superscript characters *are* used.

It is not normal to mention first editions, even if such a statement appears in
the book. Strictly speaking, if it appears you should include it, but it is not
really necessary.

Sometimes it is difficult to tell whether something is a different edition or   **1.2B3**
not. Some publishers use the word 'edition' when really all they mean is
'reprint'. If in doubt leave it out. In computer manuals and suchlike, and in
electronic resources, you may often see the word 'version' or 'revision'.

Sometimes you may need to construct an edition statement for an item
which hasn't got one, because you know that it is a new edition. You are allowed   **1.2B4**
to do this, but of course you must enclose any such statement in square
brackets.

In these cases use the same language as the title proper.   **1.2B4**

Statements of responsibility relating to the edition   **1.2C**

MARC:
250 $b
Note the
difference from
245 field.

Often a revised edition is by someone different from the original
author, and so in this case you will need to include a statement of responsibility. This is done in just the same way as in the Title and statement
of responsibility area, and has the same 'space slash space' (/) to
introduce it.

WINFIELD AND JOLOWICZ

ON

TORT

FOURTEENTH EDITION

BY

W. V. H. ROGERS, M.A.

of Gray's Inn, Barrister;
Professor of Law in the University of Leeds

First Edition	(1937) The Author
Second Edition	(1943) The Author
Third Edition	(1946) The Author
Fourth Edition	(1948) The Author
Fifth Edition	(1950) The Author
Sixth Edition	(1954) T. Ellis Lewis
Seventh Edition	(1963) J. A. Jolowicz and T. Ellis Lewis
Eighth Edition	(1967) J. A. Jolowicz with T. Ellis Lewis
Ninth Edition	(1971) J. A. Jolowicz with T. Ellis Lewis and D. M. Harris
Tenth Edition	(1975) W. V. H. Rogers
Eleventh Edition	(1979) W. V. H. Rogers
Twelfth Edition	(1984) W. V. H. Rogers
Reprinted	(1986)
Thirteenth Edition	(1989) W. V. H. Rogers
Fourteenth Edition	(1994) W. V. H. Rogers
Reprinted	(1995)

Published by
Sweet & Maxwell Limited of
South Quay Plaza, 183 Marsh Wall, London E14 9FT

title page
verso

LONDON
SWEET & MAXWELL
1994

Fig. 4.16

Examples
(Fig. 4.16, p. 55)

```
Winfield and Jolowicz on tort. - 14th ed. /
by W.V.H. Rogers
```

Notice that in this case there is no statement of responsibility in the Title and statement and responsibility area, because the only such statement relates to the edition. This is quite acceptable.

Sometimes you may have to check bibliographic sources to find out whether the name of the author has changed between editions, in order to transcribe the statement in its correct place.

(Fig. 5.10, p. 103)

```
Winward Fearon on collateral warranties /
David L. Cornes, Richard Winward. - 2nd ed.
```

Here we find that the same two authors wrote the first edition, which means that logically this statement of responsibility should come immediately after the title proper.

Sometimes you then also have to add a further statement about a reprint. **1.2D**
This is rather unusual, because it is normal to try to avoid reference to reprints, so that a catalogue record can be used unaltered by as many libraries as possible.

This is probably also the only occasion in cataloguing, or even in real life, where you put a comma at the end of one element and follow it with a capital letter at the start of the next.

Summary of Edition area
You now have further sources of information.
    Copy what is in front of you *except*

- use ordinal numerals as instructed
- abbreviate words in the main statement where possible.

Material specific details area
1.3
This is the one area which cannot be described in Chapter 1. It applies only to certain physical formats and therefore only appears as section .3 of the appropriate chapters.

The most important are in:
Chapter 3 Cartographic materials: used for *scale*   3.3
Chapter 9 Electronic resources: used for *extent and type of resource.*   9.3

MARC:
260

Publication, distribution, etc., area

1.4

In older cataloguing codes this area was often called the 'imprint'. It deals with *where*, *by whom* and *when* the item was published or otherwise issued. (Notice that in normal circumstances we are not concerned with the place or name of the *printer*.) There seems to be a lot of detail here, but in essence this is a simple area, consisting usually of just three elements:

Place of publication : Publisher, year

1.4A1

with punctuation thus, i.e. publisher introduced by 'space colon space' (:) and year introduced by 'comma space'.

Notice that again the *sources of information* which you can use will have changed, so always look at the beginning of the relevant chapter of AACR2.

1.4A2

Facsimile reprints, reproductions, etc.

1.11

If you are cataloguing a facsimile reprint, or something like a microfiche edition of something that was originally a book, remember that you are cataloguing the *reproduction*, not the original. This means that you put the *new* details here; you do not copy the details from the original title page, if that happens to have been included.

Put details of the original in the Note area.

**1.11A,
1.7B7**

The same applies if you find that the publisher's name has been changed simply because the original publisher was taken over by another one. In this case there is nothing for it but to create a new record with the new details. Again put a Note about the original publisher and date.

MARC:
260 $a

Place

1.4C1

Place normally means town or city; a state or country is not specific enough, though occasionally it may be the best you can do. Most modern commercially published books have a place of publication and there is no problem with them.

Examples
(Fig. 4.1, p. 26)

```
The art of Roman Britain / Martin Henig. -
London
```

(Fig. 4.14, p. 48)

```
Constitutional & administrative law / Helen
Fenwick. - 2nd ed. - London
```

(Fig. 4.2, p. 28)

```
The natural history of moles / Martyn L.
Gorman and R. David Stone. - London
```

The final example here shows 'London' on the title page itself, but 'Bromley' on the title page verso, and this kind of variation is more common than you might think (because the publishers know that everyone has heard of London, whereas they might not have heard of Bromley). Although you are allowed to take information in this area from *either* of those places, if you have a choice you should use the title page first because that is named first in the list of sources of information.

1.0A1, 2.0B2

There is some flexibility over whether you add the state or another qualifier after the name of the town: the rule says 'if it is considered necessary for identification, or ... to distinguish the place from others of the same name'. This results in different interpretations depending on where the catalogue record is created and on how well you know geography. An American cataloguer is likely to put

1.4C3

```
Cambridge, England
```

while a British cataloguer would put simply

```
Cambridge
```

and this illustrates one of the problems of international record exchange.

Notice also the difference in *how* the additional country, state, etc., is added, because it depends on whether or not it appears in the source of information. So the examples in AACR2 show

1.4C3

```
Carbondale, Ill.
```

and

```
Waco [Tex.]
```

In the first case the state appears in the item; in the second it does not but it has been added because it was thought useful for identification.

In any case, you must use abbreviations for such additions, though not, of course, for the place itself.

Example
(Fig. 4.3, p. 29)

```
Barbs, prongs, points, prickers & stickers :
a complete and illustrated catalogue of
antique barbed wire / Robert T. Clifton. -
Norman [Okla.]
```

Here it seems wise to add the abbreviation for Oklahoma because the word 'Norman' on its own would look strange to a British user. It goes in square brackets because it does not appear in the source of information.

1.4C3, B.14

The abbreviations of American states are those given in Appendix B; despite what you will see in many American records, it is *not* correct to use zipcodes. If the name of the state appears only in zipcode form you should replace it with the authorized abbreviation in square brackets.

B.14

Note too that there are *no abbreviations* for any of the British counties, so that if you feel a British county name is necessary you must give it *in full*.

Sometimes, especially if you are not familiar with a locality, you may find it difficult to know exactly what place to put, for example (Fig. 6.2, p. 133)

```
Houndmills, Basingstoke
```

or just

```
Basingstoke
```

It is usually safer to stick to the town unless you are quite certain that the other is a separate place. In this case

```
Basingstoke
```

is best.

Two or more places

Some books have long lists of places of publication; do we have to put them all in? The answer is no, but again this is a situation where the result will vary depending on where the catalogue record is being created. Basically you have to do three things:

MARC:
Repeat $a

- Always put the *first named* place.

  1.4C5

- Add any subsequently named place that is 'given prominence by the layout or typography of the source of information'. In practice this means *greater* prominence; i.e., it has to be made to look *more important*. This is extremely rare.

- If neither of those is in the home country of the cataloguing agency

  1.4C5

(i.e. in the country where *you* are) add the first of any named places that are in that country.

The convention is that the UK is counted as one country for this purpose. So, if you are in London and the item says 'Edinburgh and London' you need only put

```
Edinburgh
```

In all cases where you have to put more than one place, you precede each of the second and subsequent places by 'space semicolon space' (;).

Note that it is not correct to link places together with 'and', even though this may appear in the item itself. You must separate them.

Example
(Fig. 4.7, p. 37)

```
Riches of the wild : land mammals of South-
East Asia / Earl of Cranbrook ; with coloured
plates by A.M. Hughes. - Singapore ; Oxford
```

Singapore appears first, and we include Oxford because we are in Britain. An American cataloguer would put

```
Singapore ; New York
```

and ignore Oxford.

This rule, producing as it does different results depending on where the catalogue record is created, leads to difficulties in a cooperative situation. You are quite likely to be using records created in the USA, and these will show different places of publication. You should therefore establish a policy as to the extent to which you wish to amend these records to agree with British practice.

Place of publication not shown
1.4C6

In cases where the item does not show a place of publication:

- if you are *certain* of the place you should give it, but in square brackets
- if you only *fairly certain*, put a question mark as well.

Note that although normally a place-name is copied in whatever language it is, *in these cases* you give the place in *English*, even if the rest of the description is in a foreign language. Occasionally you may be able to put only a country or a state.
1.4C6

If you cannot even guess at the country, you are allowed to put

'[S.l.]', which stands for *sine loco*, i.e. 'without place' (it has a capital S simply because it is the first element in this area of the description). This should really be a *last resort*; it is not an excuse for laziness, or for stupidity in failing to work out what the place is likely to be. It is better to put a country, or even a continent, in square brackets than to have to resort to this.

Absence of a place of publication is a problem mainly in items that are not produced by major commercial publishers. Societies, galleries and suchlike quite often do not show a place of publication. If you know it, give it, but always in square brackets.

Beware of inferring a place from the name of the publisher and thus putting it without square brackets. If the place is not *explicitly* given *as a place* in one of the permitted sources of information for this area you cannot put it without square brackets.

Non-book materials

With non-book materials you are far more likely to have difficulty finding a place of publication, and this may involve some research.

Off-air recordings of radio and television programmes are a particular problem, though occasionally a place may appear at the end of the programme. You should at least usually be able to put a country in square brackets.

Remote access electronic resources are also a problem. Note the statement that you should consider them to be published, which means that you have to put something here. Sometimes the URL may give you some guidance as to the place, but usually you will need square brackets for whatever you decide to put.

9.4B2

Unpublished items

1.4C8

If the item is not published, you do not put anything for a place of publication, and do not put '[S.l.]' either. Simply omit this element.

MARC:
260 $b

Name of publisher, distributor, etc.

1.4D

Give the name of the publisher 'in the shortest form in which it can be understood and identified internationally'. This means that you should usually shorten the name as far as you can, but again remember that *only the authorized abbreviations* in Appendix B are allowed to be used.

1.4D2

Remember that the publisher is usually a corporate body and its name should therefore be capitalized according to the rules of the

**App. B
A.18,
A.39B,
etc.**

appropriate language.

Shorten the name as far as you can, including by the correct use of abbreviations. This means that if the name of the publisher ends with 'Publishing Company' you must shorten this to

```
Pub. Co.
```

and in some cases might be able to omit those words altogether.

Examples
(Fig. 4.3, p. 29)

```
Barbs, prongs, points, prickers & stickers :
a complete and illustrated catalogue of
antique barbed wire / Robert T. Clifton. -
Norman [Okla.] : University of Oklahoma Press
```

Be careful that when shortening publishers' names you do not put something misleading. For example, a University is not the same thing as its University Press. This means that whereas in most cases it would be quite permissible and correct to omit the word 'Press' at the end of a name, you should *not* do so in the case of a University Press or when it would be misleading.

(Fig. 4.6, p. 35)

```
Latin for all occasions / by Henry Beard =
Lingua Latina occasionibus omnibus / Henricus
Barbatus scripsit. - London : HarperCollins
```

Notice here that the recent tendency to run together two names, keeping a capital letter in the middle, is observed.

(Fig. 4.7, p. 37)

```
Riches of the wild : land mammals of South-
East Asia / Earl of Cranbrook ; with coloured
plates by A.M. Hughes. - Singapore ; Oxford :
Oxford University Press
```

Because only the authorized abbreviations may be used, it is not permissible to shorten this to

```
✗ : O.U.P.
```

however much you might wish to.

(Fig. 4.1, p. 26)

```
The art of Roman Britain / Martin Henig. -
London : Batsford
```

There is no need to put any more than this. As a rule of thumb, you should assume that you can *always* omit 'Ltd' if it appears in a name.

(Fig. 4.14, p. 48)

```
Constitutional & administrative law / Helen
Fenwick. - 2nd ed. - London : Cavendish
```

Again, unless there is reason to think that there are several Cavendishes, this is sufficient.

(Fig. 4.2, p. 28)

```
The natural history of moles / Martyn L.
Gorman and R. David Stone. - London :
Christopher Helm
```

This is a less well-known publisher, and it would be unwise to shorten the name further.

In shortening a publisher's name you should nevertheless retain words indicating a division within the main publisher. **1.4D3b**

Example
(Fig. 6.2, p. 133)
Not

    ✗ Basingstoke : Macmillan

but

    ✔ Basingstoke : Macmillan Education

Personally I do not see the point of this, but it is what the rule requires.

You should omit words such as 'Published by' when transcribing the name of the publisher unless it is used as a way of linking the name of the publisher with some other corporate body for which you need to make an added entry. **1.4D3**

Examples
(Fig. 4.11, p. 43)

```
Cheshire under the Norman earls : 1066-1237 /
by B.M.C. Husain ; cartography by A.G.
Hodgkiss. - Chester : Cheshire Community
Council Publications Trust
```

Notice that I have given the name of the publisher in full, including

'Publications Trust', which is presumably a subordinate part of the Cheshire Community Council. Sometimes it is clearer to put a comma after the first element of such a name, and you should do this if the nature of the name will not otherwise be clear.

(Fig. 5.9, p. 101)

```
Pre-Raphaelite drawings in the British Museum
/ J.A. Gere. - London : British Museum Press
```

In this case it is not necessary to give the whole of the statement as it appears on the title page.

What should you do about things like 'Cambridge: at the University Press'? This is a difficult question. Clearly 'Cambridge' has to be used as the *place*; this leaves very little to form the name of the publisher. I take the view that you need to put

```
Cambridge : Cambridge University Press
```

because otherwise it cannot be 'understood and identified internationally'. I may be wrong. Luckily these occurrences are rare.

Publisher part of a larger group
Most commercial publishers belong to larger groups with different names, and a book may or may not indicate this. It is not necessary to include such statements; just give the simple name of the publisher.

Examples
(Fig. 4.13, p. 47)

```
Bird census techniques / Colin J. Bibby … [et
al.] ; illustrated by Sandra Lambton, RSPB
and Simon Mustoe. - 2nd ed. - London :
Academic Press
```

The statement 'A Harcourt Science and Technology Company' on the title page is ignored.

(Fig. 5.13, p. 116)

```
The Freedom of Information Act 2000 / Michael
Supperstone, Timothy Pitt-Payne. - London :
Butterworths
```

This seems sufficient, despite the perplexing variety of names that occurs on the back of the title page.

Author as publisher

Sometimes the author is also the publisher. This may happen in the case of either a personal author or a corporate body. For a personal author, you can abbreviate the person's name to initials and surname. Names of corporate bodies should be given in the form in which they appear, but using abbreviations where possible.

B.5C

Example
(Fig. 4.4, p. 30)
```
How to avoid huge ships, or, I never met a
ship I liked / by John W. Trimmer. - Seattle
: J.W. Trimmer
```

MARC:
Repeat $b

Two or more publishers

1.4D4

The rule for these is similar to that for more than one place. Generally you do not include a second publisher except in particular circumstances, which are:

- when they are linked in a single statement
- when the first named is a distributor and a subsequently named one is the publisher
- when a subsequently named one is distinguished as the principal one by typography
- when the subsequently named one is in *your* country and the first named is not.

Sometimes you may feel this is unfair, especially when genuinely joint publication seems to be implied, but there is nothing you can do about it.

Items with no publisher

1.4D6

Again the rules have to allow for the possibility of there being no publisher, and in this case you can put '[s.n.]' for *sine nomine*. Note that unlike '[S.l.]' this does not get a capital S. This is comparatively rare.

If you have to put both '[S.l.]' and '[s.n.]' you should be put them within a single set of brackets, i.e.

1.0C1

```
[S.l. : s.n.]
```

MARC:
260 $c

Date of publication

1.4F

Usually this is straightforward, especially for printed books. You just give the year.

1.4F1

If the year appears in roman numerals convert them to arabic.

1.4F1

If you know that the date is wrong, you should add the correct date in square brackets after copying the date as shown. This usually only arises either because the date is misprinted or because the printer is deliberately trying to disguise something.

1.4F2

Sometimes a book comes out some time after the date which has been printed in it, and sometimes it may be before. It is still quite common to print the following year's date in books which are being published towards the end of the year, and it does not help anyone in the long run if you 'correct' these, because citations to them will always contain the date actually printed in the book.

Do not include the month even if it appears.

The date you give should always be the date of the *edition*, and should relate to the information given in the Edition area, if any.

1.4F1

Examples
(Fig. 4.7, p. 37)

```
Riches of the wild : land mammals of South-
East Asia / Earl of Cranbrook ; with coloured
plates by A.M. Hughes. - Singapore ; Oxford :
Oxford University Press, 1987
```

(Fig. 4.1, p. 26)

```
The art of Roman Britain / Martin Henig. -
London : Batsford, 1995
```

(Fig. 4.14, p. 48)

```
Constitutional & administrative law / Helen
Fenwick. - 2nd ed. - London : Cavendish, 1995
```

Notice that here the date is that of the second edition.

(Fig. 4.11, p. 43)

```
Cheshire under the Norman earls : 1066-1237 /
by B.M.C. Husain ; cartography by A.G.
Hodgkiss. - Chester : Cheshire Community
Council Publications Trust, 1973
```

Copyright dates

1.4F5

It is possible to include a copyright date: notice that the abbreviation for this is 'c' which is closed up to the date itself. This is not very helpful for catalogue users, who are unlikely to know what it means.

If the item has '© 2001' in it, but not a specific statement that it was published in 2001, what should you put? For a British book it is normally adequate to put

```
        , 2001
```

rather than

```
        , c2001
```

because in the UK books do not normally have copyright dates which differ from their date of publication. In the USA where copyright is not obtained automatically but has to be registered there is more likelihood of the dates differing.

Examples
(Fig. 4.3, p. 29)

```
        Barbs, prongs, points, prickers & stickers : a
        complete and illustrated catalogue of antique
        barbed wire / Robert T. Clifton. - Norman
        [Okla.] : University of Oklahoma Press, c1970
```

This is probably technically better than just

```
        , 1970
```

though that would be acceptable.

(Fig. 4.2, p. 28)
```
        The natural history of moles / Martyn L.
        Gorman and R. David Stone. - London :
        Christopher Helm, 1990
```

Dates of printing

It is normal to ignore reprints and just include the date of the edition; AACR2 does not suggest mentioning a reprint date unless it is the only date that can be found.

1.4F6

In a cooperative situation it would be particularly unhelpful to mention reprint dates, because it would mean that a library with a different reprint would not be able to make use of the same catalogue record.

Items without dates

1.4F7

Most commercially published books have a date of publication, but less mainstream material may sometimes lack a date. The important thing to realize is that whereas '[S.l.]' and '[s.n.]' exist there is *no such equivalent* for 'no date'; you *must* make a guess and put something. The examples show you the kinds of thing you can put.

If you need to put an approximate date the abbreviation for circa ('about') is 'ca.', not just 'c.'. Remember to include the square brackets.

Beware of treating something as a date of publication when it is not explicitly stated to be such. For example, an art exhibition catalogue may give the date of the exhibition but not explicitly the date of publication of the catalogue. In this case you need to put the date in square brackets because it is not explicitly stated as being the date of publication.

If you are creating a single record to catalogue a multipart item you are allowed to put the first and last dates in the sequence.

1.4F8

Summary of Publication, distribution, etc. area

Again be careful of sources of information. Give three elements:

Place
- always first place
- + another given prominence
- + another in own country

Publisher
- shorten name as far as practicable

Year of publication
- there is *no abbreviation* for 'no date'.

MARC:
300

Physical description area

1.5

Here we have potentially four elements:

- extent of item
- other physical details
- dimensions
- accompanying material.

The nature of these naturally varies considerably depending on what physical form of material you are cataloguing. We shall first continue to concentrate on printed books, and it is therefore more useful to use AACR2 Chapter 2 to look at this area in detail. This translates the first three of these elements into

- number of volumes and/or pagination   2.5B
- illustrative matter   2.5C
- dimensions.   2.5D

Accompanying material remains as the fourth element, but it is much   2.5E less frequently used than the first three.

We shall now look at each of these in turn. Not all the details are covered here, and you should look at the full rules to see what I have missed out.

Obviously I cannot reproduce whole books here so that you can count the pages and look at the pictures, so you will just have to take my word for the details that I put in, and use them as examples. You can, however, use this book itself as an example.

Number of volumes and/or pagination

Although 'Number of volumes' is mentioned first, for *books* it is used *only* when dealing with multi-volume works. For single-volume works the most commonly needed piece of information is the number of pages in the book.

2.5B16, 2.5B17

2.5B1

Non-book materials

For non-book materials the number of items is included in all cases: e.g.

```
1 globe
6 maps
1 sound cassette
1 videocassette
2 film cassettes
1 computer disk
```

3.5B1, 6.5B1, 7.5B1, 9.5B1

But note that for electronic resources available only by remote access (websites, etc.) you do not give a physical description at all. That means that the whole of this area is omitted.

9.5

The rules on number of pages may look rather complicated, but that is because they have to cater for many exceptional cases. Most books are straightforward: you just give the *last numbered* page, followed by a space and 'p.'.

2.5B2

If there are some unnumbered pages (even *after* the final numbered one) you can ignore them unless they constitute a substantial amount; you are not trying to account for every page in the book. If you do have to mention unnumbered pages, you either

2.5B3

- give the exact number in square brackets or
- give an approximate number preceded by 'ca.', *without* square brackets.

2.5B3

Obviously you do whichever is more convenient.

If there is a roman sequence at the beginning, you give the last numbered in that sequence too. This applies to any other separate sequences that there may be. Separate each sequence with 'comma space'.

2.5B2

Convert roman sequences in capital letters to lower case.

C.2B3

If there is a roman sequence you need to check that the arabic numbers do indeed start again at 1. If they simply run on from the roman sequence, you ignore the roman sequence altogether and just give the final number of the arabic.

2.5B5

You may notice that several of the examples in AACR2 refer to 'leaves', not 'pages'. The difference is that leaves are printed on only one side; otherwise you should usually refer to pages.

2.5B2,
2.5B3,
etc.

Examples

(Fig. 4.1, p. 26)

```
The art of Roman Britain / Martin Henig. -
London : Batsford, 1995. - 224 p.
```

(Fig. 4.2, p. 28)

```
The natural history of moles / Martyn L.
Gorman and R. David Stone. - London :
Christopher Helm, 1990. - xiv, 138 p.
```

(Fig. 4.3, p. 29)

```
Barbs, prongs, points, prickers & stickers :
a complete and illustrated catalogue of
antique barbed wire / Robert T. Clifton. -
Norman [Okla.] : University of Oklahoma
Press, c1970. - xxi, 418 p.
```

(This book)

```
Essential cataloguing / J.H. Bowman. - London
: Facet, 2003. - viii, 216 p.
```

The commonest addition that you need to make to the number of pages is where there are *plates*. You add the number of *pages* of plates (which may or may not be the number of *individual* plates) after the other numbers of pages that you have already given. If the pages of the plates are not actually numbered, you need to give the number of pages that they amount to in square brackets.

2.5B9

Sometimes it is difficult to know what constitutes a plate. It is easiest to think of them as pages of illustrations which are usually printed on a different kind of paper *and which are not numbered as part of the main page-numbering sequence of the book.*

Example

(Fig. 4.1, p. 26)

```
The art of Roman Britain / Martin Henig. -
London : Batsford, 1995. - 224 p., [8] p. of
plates
```

Errors in pagination   2.5B4

If something is clearly wrong with the number of the page that you are copying out, you should correct it, *after copying* it first. There may be a simple misprint, or the book may be numbered in such a way that the final number would be confusing.

Non-book materials

Non-book materials do not have pages, but there is usually an equivalent, the difference from books being that this time the information goes in parentheses.

For an atlas you put the number of pages in the same way as for a book, e.g.

```
1 atlas (xvi, 97, 100 p.)
```
3.5C2

In the case of any kind of recording it is the number of minutes' playing time.

```
1 sound cassette (30 min.)
1 videocassette (25 min.)
2 film cassettes (30 min. each)
```
6.5B2

7.5B2

See the full rules for further detail.

Illustrative matter   2.5C

This element is preceded by 'space colon space' (:).   2.5A1

If the book has no illustrations you just ignore this element and go on to the next. Do not leave a gap.

Otherwise put 'ill.' for any kind of illustration.   2.5C1

Optionally, you may specify certain kinds of illustration if you consider them   2.5C2
important, in which case you use the appropriate abbreviations from Appen-   **App. B**
dix B.

If you do this, photographs do not count as a special kind of illustration, presumably because they are too common.

Coloured illustrations should be described as 2.5C3

```
: col. ill.
```

This is not optional.

Obviously books have varying proportions of coloured illustrations 2.5C3
amid otherwise black and white ones. You will therefore sometimes need
to put

```
: ill. (chiefly col.)
```

or

```
: ill. (some col.)
```

Notice that you should give the *number* of illustrations if it 'can be ascer- 2.5C4
tained readily'. This is often forgotten. Clearly if all the illustrations
are numbered this is easy to do, whereas if it would involve counting
a large number it would not be necessary.

Always think of the catalogue users, and how they may be helped by
the information you provide.

Examples
(Fig. 4.1, p. 26)

```
The art of Roman Britain / Martin Henig. -
London : Batsford, 1995. - 224 p., [8] p. of
plates : 125 ill. (16 col.)
```

Here the illustrations are numbered throughout, and the 16 coloured
ones are easily identifiable.

(Fig. 4.3, p. 29)

```
Barbs, prongs, points, prickers & stickers :
a complete and illustrated catalogue of
antique barbed wire / Robert T. Clifton. -
Norman [Okla.] : University of Oklahoma
Press, c1970. - xxi, 418 p. : 992 ill.
```

It may seem strange to give such a large and precise number of illustrations, but it is easily ascertainable, and so there is no excuse for not
including it.

Sometimes beginners wonder whether they need to mention illustrations if they have already said that there are plates. The answer is Yes,
because this is a separate element of the physical description. In the first
element you are giving an account of the number of physical pages in

the book. In the second you are indicating whether there are any illustrations. Because these are quite separate aspects, you need to mention both, even if it seems like duplication of information.

Notice that 'tables containing only words and/or numbers are not illustrations', and that you can also disregard 'minor' illustrations.

2.5C1

Non-book materials

For cartographic materials there is a strong correspondence with books, in that you indicate whether the map is coloured; there are also details about its mounting.

3.5C

For sound recordings this element is used for the type of recording and playing speed, and certain other playing characteristics, e.g.

6.5C

```
: analog, 33 rpm
```

Videos show 'sd.' or 'si.' for 'sound' or 'silent', and also indicate presence of colour, e.g.

7.5C

```
: sd., col.
```

Again see the rules for fuller information.

Dimensions

This is the third element of this area, and for books it generally means the *height* of the book when standing on the shelf; it is therefore its *outside* dimension, not the size of the pages. You give the height in centimetres, rounded *up* to the next whole centimetre.

2.5D1

Examples

(Fig. 4.1, p. 26)

```
The art of Roman Britain / Martin Henig. -
London : Batsford, 1995. - 224 p., [8] p. of
plates : 125 ill. (16 col.) ; 25 cm.
```

(Fig. 4.2, p. 28)

```
The natural history of moles / Martyn L.
Gorman and R. David Stone. - London :
Christopher Helm, 1990. - xiv, 138 p. : ill.
(some col.) ; 24 cm.
```

(Fig. 4.3, p. 29)

```
Barbs, prongs, points, prickers & stickers : a
complete and illustrated catalogue of antique
barbed wire / Robert T. Clifton. - Norman
[Okla.] : University of Oklahoma Press, c1970.
- xxi, 418 p. : 992 ill. ; 19 cm.
```

(This book)

```
Essential cataloguing / J.H. Bowman. - London
: Facet, 2003. - viii, 216 p. : ill. ; 25 cm.
```

Optionally, you could put

```
: ill., facsims.
```

here, because most of the illustrations are title page facsimiles.

The only exceptions to this are:

- unusually small books, less than 10 cm., in which case you give the height in millimetres   **2.5D1**
- books of unusual shape, either
  — those which are wider than they are tall, or
  — those whose height is more than double their width,   **2.5D2**
- in which case you give the height × the width.

The thing to remember is that the *height*, which is the element that is *always* included, comes first.

Non-book materials

For maps give the dimensions, as height × width.   **3.5D**

    For sound recordings the kind of dimension given here will vary   **6.5D** with the format, e.g. the size of a sound disc, or the width of a tape in a sound cassette *if not standard*.

    For videos give the width of the tape in inches or millimetres.   **7.5D**

Accompanying material   **2.5E**

This is the fourth element of this area, and it is comparatively rarely needed. It is used for things like an accompanying disc, or perhaps for a leaflet that accompanies a multi-media package; the main thing about it is that whatever is referred to is *detachable* or *loose*. Some libraries may prefer to catalogue such things separately.

    It is separated from the previous element by 'space plus-sign space' (+), which at least has the virtue of being logical, as it refers to something additional.

> **Summary of Physical description area**
>
> Three main elements:
>
> - extent of item (for books, pages)
> - whether illustrated
> - dimension(s) (for books, height).
>
> plus occasionally, accompanying material.

Series area

<table>
<tr><td>

MARC:
440 or 490
See Chapter 5
(pp. 127–9) for
more inform-
ation on which
tag to use, and
for series added
entries.

</td><td>

We can now return to AACR2 Chapter 1 to look at series. For a fuller discussion of the differences between series and multipart items see my Chapter 6 (pp. 129–34). All series statements appear in parentheses; this is part of AACR's standard punctuation. If there is more than one series statement each one goes in its own set of parentheses.

</td></tr>
</table>

1.6

1.6A1

In a computerized system you will probably find that you do not need to put in the parentheses as they can be generated automatically.

Bear in mind that for most physical formats you again have a different source of information, allowing greater scope than for the Title and statement of responsibility area.

In other respects, however, this area is rather like the Title and statement of responsibility area, in that in addition to the title proper it may contain

<table>
<tr><td>

repeat $a
no coding
no coding

</td><td>

- parallel title
- other title information
- statements of responsibility.

</td></tr>
</table>

It may also include

<table>
<tr><td>

$x
$v
$n for numeric
subseries,
$p for name of
subseries

</td><td>

- ISSN
- numbering within series
- subseries.

Again you are *copying* what is in front of you, but there are some fresh exceptions, as follows:

</td></tr>
</table>

- Do *not* include other title information *unless* it 'provides valuable information identifying the series'.
- Likewise, do not include statements of responsibility unless they are 'considered to be necessary for identifying the series'.

1.6D

1.6E

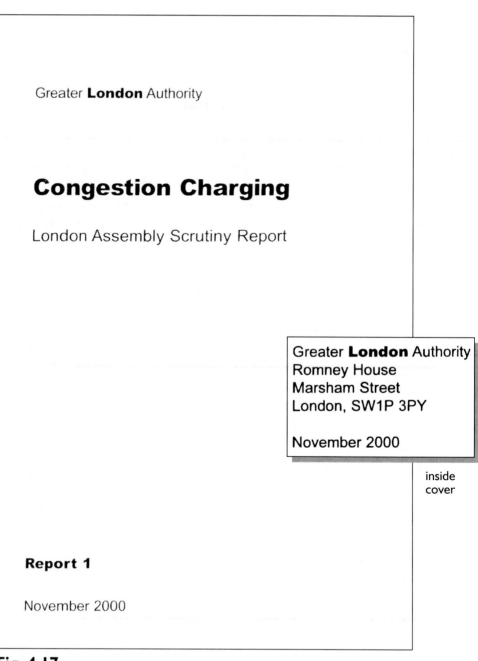

Greater **London** Authority

Congestion Charging

London Assembly Scrutiny Report

Greater **London** Authority
Romney House
Marsham Street
London, SW1P 3PY

November 2000

inside
cover

Report 1

November 2000

Fig. 4.17

This means that in most cases you will omit both of these elements when they occur.

Example

(Fig. 4.2, p. 28)

```
The natural history of moles / Martyn L.
Gorman and R. David Stone. - London :
Christopher Helm, 1990. - xiv, 138 p. : ill.
(some col.) ; 24 cm. - (Christopher Helm
mammal series)
```

Here we ignore the statement 'Edited by Dr Ernest Neal, MBE, former President of the Mammal Society'.

(Fig. 4.10, p. 42)

```
Melchanolies [sic] of knowledge : literature
in the age of science / edited by Margery
Arent Safir. - Albany, N.Y. : State
University of New York Press, 1999. - ix, 205
p. ; 23 cm. - (The margins of literature)
```

In this case it seems reasonable to treat 'SUNY series' as other title information, even though it precedes what is apparently the title proper of the series, because it is not grammatically linked to it. It can therefore be omitted.

The main occasion for including a statement of responsibility is when the series title proper is of a very vague or general nature, such as 'Research paper', which is not very helpful unless you know *whose* research paper it is.

Example

(Fig. 4.17, opposite)

```
Congestion charging : London Assembly
scrutiny report. - London : Greater London
Authority, 2000. - 1 v. in various pagings :
col. ill. ; 30 cm. - (Report ; 1)
```

This series statement is rather useless on its own, and it might be better to combine it with the statement at the head of the title to make a series statement with a statement of responsibility, thus:

```
(Report / Greater London Authority ; 1)
```

Sometimes beginners are doubtful about whether the word 'series' itself should be included in the series statement. This entirely depends on how the information is presented in the item. If the word 'series' appears to be part of the series title, include it; otherwise not. If different sources of information show different versions, follow the order of precedence for sources of information in this area.

1.0A1, 2.0B2, etc.

MARC: 440/490 $x

ISSN

1.6F

Some series have an ISSN (International Standard Serial Number), and this comes next, preceded by 'comma space' and including the letters 'ISSN'. This applies mainly to the kinds of series whose individual volumes come out regularly and for which you might wish to enter a standing order. Most ordinary book series do not have ISSNs.

MARC: 440/490 $v

Numbering within series

1.6G

Not all series have numbers, so don't worry if there isn't one. If there is a number, however, you include it, preceding it with 'space semicolon space' (;). Use the terminology of the item itself: this means that if the series refers to 'volumes' you put 'v.', and if it has 'numbers' you put 'no.', or whatever is the appropriate abbreviation in a foreign language.

1.6A1 B.9

Note that 'volume' is abbreviated to 'v.' *unless* the result would be unclear (usually because of a roman numeral: see below), in which case you put 'vol.'.

B.9 fn. 10

If the item has a number but does not use any term like 'volume' or 'number' you simply put the number without any abbreviated term.

In all cases numbers should be converted into arabic numerals, with the exception that roman numerals can be retained if the result would otherwise be unclear.

C.2B1, C.2B2

Sometimes the series statement and volume number are not presented in a conventional or convenient way. Unfortunately, because in this area you have to *copy* what is in front of you, you cannot change anything round.

Example
(Fig. 4.11, p. 43)

```
Cheshire under the Norman earls : 1066-1237 /
by B.M.C. Husain ; cartography by A.G.
Hodgkiss. - Chester : Cheshire Community
Council Publications Trust, 1973. - xi, 142
p., [4] p. of plates : ill., maps ; 24 cm. -
(Volume four of a history of Cheshire)
```

You cannot turn it round to

✗ (A history of Cheshire ; v. 4)

What you can do, however, is make an added entry for the series in a more appropriate form (see p. 127).

Subseries

1.6H

MARC:
440/490
$n for numeric subseries,
$p for name of subseries

A series can be divided into subseries, and you can add the appropriate wording, preceded by 'full stop space', and starting with a fresh capital letter.

Examples
(Fig. 5.11, p. 111)

```
Great expectations / Charles Dickens ; retold
by Florence Bell. - Oxford : Heinemann ELT,
1993. - 95 p. : ill. ; 20 cm. - (Heinemann
ELT guided readers. Upper level)
```

(Fig. 8.1, p. 156)
```
Advances in artificial intelligence : 12th
Biennial Conference of the Canadian Society
for Computational Studies of Intelligence,
AI'98, Vancouver, BC, Canada, June 18-20,
1998 : proceedings. - Berlin ; London :
Springer, 1998. - xii, 466 p : ill. ; 24 cm.
- (Lecture notes in computer science. Lecture
notes in artificial intelligence ; 1418)
```

Summary of Series area
Generally, like Title and statement of responsibility area, except:

- different sources of information
- normally omit other title information
- normally omit statement of responsibility.

Remember abbreviations in number element, and normally convert roman numerals to arabic.

Note area

1.7

MARC:
500-586
Consult a MARC 21 manual for further information

In looking at this area we are moving to a different kind of information. We are no longer necessarily *copying* from a particular source of information, because we can 'take data recorded in notes from any suitable source'. This means that we are free to make up notes in any way we think fit, and we can take information from anywhere we like.

It follows from this that square brackets are not used in notes, except for 'interpolations within quoted material'. This is often forgotten.   1.7A2

Form of notes
Order of information   1.7A3
Although you can take information from any source you like, there are still some rules as to how you should set a note out. The main thing to remember is that if you are giving the kind of information which is similar to what might appear in one of the other areas of description you should set it out in the same way.

This means, for example, that if you need to make a note about a different edition of a book, you give the details in the same order

```
Place : Publisher, year
```

as you would if you were in the Publication, distribution, etc. area itself.

Quotations   1.7A3
Sometimes the most convenient way of conveying the information is to make a direct quotation from some other source. There are two important things to notice about this:

- Use *double* quotation marks
- Give the source of your quotation after it, *unless the source is the chief source of information of the item.*

This means that if you wish to quote something from the title page of a book, you do *not* indicate where the quotation comes from, and this very fact shows that it must be from the title page.

Formal and informal notes   1.7A3
You should always write your notes as concisely as possible. Do not ramble. Look at the examples given in AACR2 and follow them.

MARC:
Use 500 for each kind except where a different tag is shown.

Different kinds of note   1.7B
What kinds of thing should you make a note about? Generally, you make notes on matters which you think are important but which do not fit neatly into any other area of the description. Have a look at the examples given in AACR2 and you will soon get an idea of the kinds of thing meant.

Nature, scope or artistic form

This is fairly self-explanatory, though I have seldom seen it used. In theory there is no reason why it should not be used to indicate literary form, but conventionally it does not seem to be.

MARC:
546

Language

1.7B2

You would not normally indicate the language of the main text of an item, because this should be evident from the title, but it is often useful to mention that some parts of the work are in a different language, or to show that the work is a translation from another language. You might also wish to indicate that a work has parallel titles in different languages.

Source of title proper

1.7B3

If you have to use a source other than the chief source of information, you must put a note here to indicate where you have taken the title from.

Variations in title

1.7B4

Related to the previous one, this kind of note allows you to mention variant titles. Quite often a book will have a shorter title on the spine or cover, and because this is the first part of the book that the user will see it is useful to indicate what it says.

Parallel titles and other title information

1.7B5

Sometimes you may wish to include information for which there is not room in the normal area of description. This is most likely to occur when Other title information is very long, or when something appears on the cover but not in the chief source of information.

Statements of responsibility

1.7B6

If it is important to mention a person or body as being responsible for some aspect of the item, and you cannot include it in the appropriate statement because it does not appear in the 'correct' source of information, you can always add it in a note.

This is quite common in books, where you may find the name of a corporate body appearing on the title page, but not directly connected to the rest of the Title and statement of responsibility area. If you feel that it ought to be mentioned, and especially if you think it deserves an access point, you can mention it in a note.

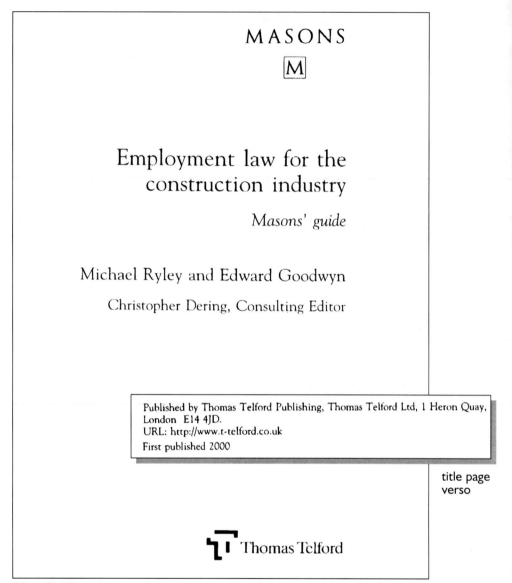

MASONS

M

Employment law for the
construction industry

Masons' guide

Michael Ryley and Edward Goodwyn

Christopher Dering, Consulting Editor

Published by Thomas Telford Publishing, Thomas Telford Ltd, 1 Heron Quay, London E14 4JD.
URL: http://www.t-telford.co.uk
First published 2000

title page
verso

Thomas Telford

Fig. 4.18

Examples
(Fig. 4.18)

```
Employment law for the construction industry
/ Michael Ryley and Edward Goodwyn ;
Christopher Dering, consulting editor. -
London : Thomas Telford, 2000. - xiv, 157 p.
; 22 cm. - (Masons' guide). - At head of
title: Masons
```

(Fig. 4.8, p. 38)

```
Rabbit hutches on postage stamps : economics,
planning and development in the 1990s / Alan
Evans. - [Cambridge?] : Granta Editions,
c1990. - 25 p. ; 21 cm. - (The 12th Denman
lecture, 1990). - "University of Cambridge,
Department of Land Economy"
```

This note is perhaps rather odd, and less than ideal. But it does convey, to the initiated, that these words appear on the title page. The only reason for including them at all is to provide justification for making an added entry under the heading for the Department.

It is not certain that the Series statement should be as it is; another possibility would be to include it as a second piece of other title information.

Notice also that on this occasion I have marked the copyright date as such. This is because there is a possibility that the lecture, though delivered in 1990, was not actually published in that year.

Edition and history   1.7B7

This is quite common. The convention is that, when you are cataloguing a later edition than the first, you make a note about the *immediately preceding* edition. You do not go further back than that; you are not trying to create a complete bibliographical history of the work.

Similarly, if you are cataloguing a reprint of a work which was previously published by a different publisher, you will give the details of the edition of which it is a reprint.

In either case, you give enough details to allow the catalogue user to identify the edition concerned. This means that if the place and publisher are the same, you need only give the date. If the publisher is different, you will need to give place, publisher and date.

Examples
(Fig. 4.6, p. 35)

```
Latin for all occasions / by Henry Beard =
Lingua Latina occasionibus omnibus / Henricus
Barbatus scripsit. - London : HarperCollins,
1993. - xviii, 91 p. : ill. ; 21 cm. - First
British ed.: London : Angus & Robertson, 1991
```

There are different possible ways of doing this note, and we might mention the original American edition, which is not referred to in the book itself. Notice that 'London' is not mentioned in this edition as the place of publication in connexion with Angus & Robertson, but we do *not* use square brackets because they are not required in the Note area.

(Fig. 4.14, p. 48)

```
Constitutional & administrative law / Helen
Fenwick. - 2nd ed. - London : Cavendish,
1995. - xvi, 365 p. ; 22 cm. - (The
Cavendish Q & A series). - Previous ed.:
1993
```

Here there is no need to show the place and publisher of the previous edition because they are the same as for this one.

Do not apply this rule in the case of authors like Shakespeare, whose works have been published in numerous editions. Only give details of the previous edition by the same publisher. No one wants you to give details of when a Shakespeare play was first published.

Most of the remaining kinds of note are seldom needed, but you can use them if you need to:

• Material (or type of publication) specific details	**1.7B8**
• Publication, distribution, etc.	**1.7B9**
• Physical description	**1.7B10**
• Accompanying material and supplements	**1.7B11**
• Series	**1.7B12**
• Audience	**1.7B14**
• Reference to published descriptions	**1.7B15**

Two should be picked out as being more common.

MARC: 502

Dissertations   **1.7B13**

Of all these kinds of note this is probably the most commonly used, as so many dissertations are subsequently published as books.

Remember that if you are cataloguing a dissertation itself you will not include any publication information in the Publication etc. area.   **1.4C8, 1.4D8**

MARC: 504 for bibliographies and indexes; 505 for other contents. It is possible to use the first indicator to generate an introductory word such as 'Contents:'.

Contents   **1.7B18, 2.7B18**

This kind of note can take a variety of forms. It is used mainly

• to mention bibliographies and indexes; many libraries ignore this
• to list individual works which are included in one physical item; this is normally done only for works which exist separately in their own right. It would not be done for chapter titles, for example.

Standard number and terms of availability area   1.8

There is no point in spending much time on this, because in most systems it would probably be ignored. The ISBN is usually used as the control number for the catalogue record, and it is therefore input at an earlier stage.

If you do need to use this field, note that again you can take information from *any source*. ISBNs should be preceded by the letters 'ISBN' and should then be set out as they appear in the item, that is, with either hyphens or spaces. (There is no difference between hyphens and spaces; it is just that different publishers use different methods of separating the elements in the ISBN.)

Additions to standard numbers   1.8E1

You are permitted to add qualifications to a standard number to show the binding format of the item, or the country in which the ISBN applies.

5 Access points

The whole of AACR2 Chapter 21 is devoted to access points, formerly often known as entry points; that is, it deals with the question of who or what is going to get an access point in the catalogue. As I mentioned earlier, AACR2 still maintains the distinction between *main entry* and *added entries*; if it did not do so, most of this chapter could be swept away, because all access points would be equal. In an online catalogue they are effectively equal anyway, but as long as the rules remain as they are we need to understand how they work.

21.0A1

Online catalogues also usually provide various other kinds of access points which are not mentioned by AACR2 at all, such as Keyword and Publisher. And remember that AACR2 does not deal with subject access in any way.

As with so many sections of AACR2, the basics are very simple, but they can often be obscured by the detail which is necessary to deal with unusual cases.

The first thing to note is that, unlike in the description, we are no longer tied closely to particular *sources of information* in the item itself; although the item itself naturally still has priority, we are allowed to use external sources if required. The order of sources is

21.0B1

- chief source of information
- statements prominently stated (remember what 'prominently' means)
- information in the content of the item
- information from outside the item.

0.8

In practice this seldom makes any difference, but, for example, in the case of an anonymous work whose authorship has subsequently been established, it does allow us to make the entry under the actual author's name even though it does not appear in the item itself.

The next thing is that, because AACR2 breaks down the task of cataloguing into as many separate operations as possible, the actual *form* of the access points is not discussed at all in this chapter. As I said at the

21.0C1

beginning (pp. 12–13), there is a difference between deciding that Shakespeare is going to be the main entry and establishing the actual form of his name that we are going to use. This means that whenever an access point is referred to in AACR2 Chapter 21, the *actual form* of the access point cannot be mentioned because that is dealt with in other chapters. Instead a circumlocution is always used, which is why all the references are expressed like '*Main entry under the heading for Hemingway*', because at this stage we are not concerned with *what* the form of heading for Hemingway will be.

You should disregard the optional 'designations of function'; they are seldom used. | **21.0D1**

The next rule is the **most important in the whole book**, and also for many the most difficult to understand. It is broken into three sections: | **21.1**

- Works of personal authorship | **21.1A**
- Entry under corporate body | **21.1B**
- Entry under title | **21.1C**

which between them cover all the possibilities for access points. We shall look at each of these in turn.

Note, first, the contrast between the ways in which the first two are expressed. It is recognized that 'authorship' can be personal, whereas, although some items may be entered under corporate body, the term 'authorship' is not thought appropriate for them. | **21.1A, 21.1B**

Next note the definitions of 'personal author' and 'corporate body'.

Personal author

Personal author is quite straightforward, being the 'person chiefly responsible for the creation of the intellectual or artistic content of a work'. Normally this presents no problems: it is a way of eliminating editors of collections of papers, because they are not responsible for the intellectual content. | **21.1A1**

Examples
Returning to our examples from the previous chapter, we can see some simple cases where just one author is involved:
(Fig. 4.1, p. 26)

```
The art of Roman Britain / Martin Henig
```

Main entry under the heading for Henig.

(Fig. 4.3, p. 29)

```
Barbs, prongs, points, prickers & stickers :
a complete and illustrated catalogue of
antique barbed wire / Robert T. Clifton
```

Main entry under the heading for Clifton.

(Fig. 4.4, p. 30)

```
How to avoid huge ships, or, I never met a
ship I liked / by John W. Trimmer
```

Main entry under the heading for Trimmer.

Beware of certain items that may contain a person's name but are *not* the result of that person's work. This applies particularly to things like lists of an artist's work in an exhibition.

We can pass over rule **21.1A2** for the moment; all its provisions are expanded on in the rest of the chapter. **21.1A2**

Corporate body

Entry under corporate body is less straightforward. We have to consider two questions: **21.1B1**

- Are we dealing with a corporate body at all?
- Is the corporate body the main entry?

1. Are we dealing with a corporate body?

The definition of 'corporate body' means that the first thing to keep in mind is that a corporate body *must have a name*. If it has no name, then however much you may think it is a corporate body, it cannot count as one for the purposes of this rule.

For many organizations, such as societies, institutions, museums, business firms, and so on, there is usually no difficulty. We are all familiar with them, and we recognize them as corporate bodies.

The problem arises mostly in the case of conferences, which are mentioned at the end of the first paragraph of the rule, and with the kinds of thing mentioned in the final paragraph: athletic contests, exhibitions, and so on. Most ordinary people would probably not think of a conference, an athletic contest, or an exhibition as being a corporate body at all, and you really need to get yourself in the correct frame of mind, so that you realize that *in the right circumstances* such a thing can be a corporate body. **21.1B1**

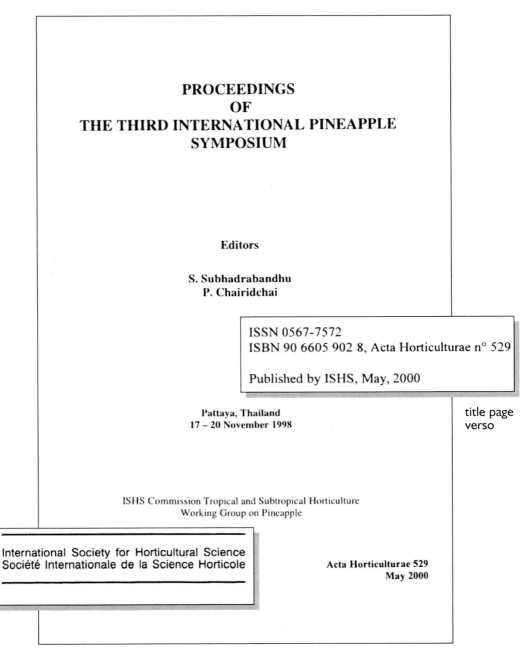

PROCEEDINGS
OF
THE THIRD INTERNATIONAL PINEAPPLE
SYMPOSIUM

Editors

S. Subhadrabandhu
P. Chairidchai

ISSN 0567-7572
ISBN 90 6605 902 8, Acta Horticulturae n° 529

Published by ISHS, May, 2000

Pattaya, Thailand
17 – 20 November 1998

title page
verso

ISHS Commission Tropical and Subtropical Horticulture
Working Group on Pineapple

International Society for Horticultural Science
Société Internationale de la Science Horticole

ISHS

Acta Horticulturae 529
May 2000

page
opposite
title page

Fig. 5.1

CONTEMPORARY MATHEMATICS

188

Homotopy Theory and Its Applications

A Conference on Algebraic Topology
in Honor of Samuel Gitler
August 9–13, 1993
Cocoyoc, Mexico

Alejandro Adem
R. James Milgram
Douglas C. Ravenel
Editors

A conference on Algebraic Topology was held at Cocoyoc, Mexico, August 9 13, 1993.

title page
verso

American Mathematical Society
Providence, Rhode Island

Fig. 5.2

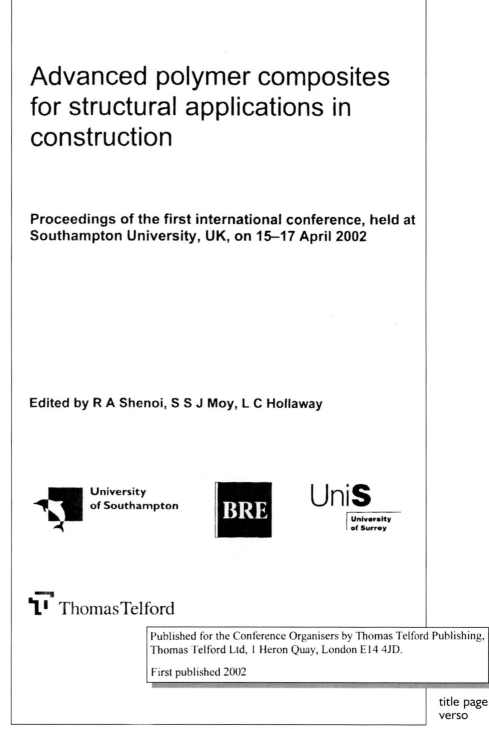

Advanced polymer composites for structural applications in construction

Proceedings of the first international conference, held at Southampton University, UK, on 15–17 April 2002

Edited by R A Shenoi, S S J Moy, L C Hollaway

University of Southampton

BRE

UniS University of Surrey

 ThomasTelford

Published for the Conference Organisers by Thomas Telford Publishing, Thomas Telford Ltd, 1 Heron Quay, London E14 4JD.

First published 2002

title page verso

Fig. 5.3

The right circumstances are, of course, that it has a *name*. How do you tell? We are given a little guidance on how to decide whether a body has a name. A body has a name if

21.1B1

- in a language that uses capital letters for corporate bodies it has capital letters; or
- in a language using articles, the words are always associated with a definite article (see Appendix E for articles in different languages).

App. E

This is helpful to some extent, but it does not always get us all the way. Luckily it usually works for English.

The commonest occasion for needing to decide carefully whether something has a name is with respect to *conferences*. Some conferences have a very clearly stated name, like 'The Third International Pineapple Symposium' (Fig. 5.1, p. 89), while others simply state that they are 'a conference on ...', usually giving the dates and place (Fig. 5.2, p. 90). The definite article is usually the defining factor. It is vital to establish whether a conference has a name, because this will affect your choice of rules to apply in cataloguing it.

Sometimes the definite article is *not* enough, because what remains is not sufficient to constitute a name. So in Fig. 5.3 (p. 91) the conference does *not* have a name, because 'the first international conference' is not distinctive enough as a name, and no fuller name appears elsewhere in the publication.

2. Can the corporate body be the main entry?

21.1B2

Having established that what we are dealing with is a corporate body, we can proceed to the next part of the rule, which is the crux of the whole thing and the part that beginners find the hardest thing in AACR2 to understand. We shall look at what it says step by step.

First, the item must 'emanate' from the corporate body, and we are given a definition of emanating in footnote 2. A work emanates from a corporate body if it

21.1B2 fn. 2

- is issued by that body; or
- has been caused to be issued by that body; or
- originated with that body.

If none of these apply, then we can forget about corporate bodies, and we need read no further in this rule.

But assuming that we get over this hurdle, and that the item *does emanate* from a corporate body, we then have to consider whether it falls within any of the subdivisions (a) to (f) of the rule. You need to read

21.1B2 a–f

Patron: Her Majesty the Queen
Established 2002
Incorporated by Royal Charter 1898

CILIP: the Chartered Institute of Library and Information Professionals

YEARBOOK 2002–2003

Compiled by

Kathryn Beecroft

facet publishing

Fig. 5.4

these subdivisions very carefully.

In practice you can usually eliminate

(b) certain legal, governmental and religious works	**21.1B2**
(e) certain works resulting from performances; and	**b, e, f**
(f) cartographic materials	

because they relate to very specific types of material which are obvious when you see them; but remember that they are there in case you need them.

It is (a), (c) and (d) which are most often relevant. Let us look at these first.

(a) those of an administrative nature dealing with the corporate body itself, etc.

21.1B2a

The commonest examples here are things like membership lists, year-books of organizations, catalogues of collections. The difficulty lies in the words 'of an administrative nature'. You would hardly think that a published catalogue of the contents of a museum, for example, was 'of an administrative nature'. I can only say that if you look at the examples that follow on subsequent pages of AACR2 you will see that such catalogues are invariably entered in this way, and the words 'of an administrative nature' seem to be disregarded. Indeed, it is hard to see what the words mean or what difference they might make.

21.4A, 21.4B

Examples
(Fig. 5.4, p. 93)

```
Yearbook 2002-2003 / CILIP: the Chartered
Institute of Library and Information
Professionals ; compiled by Kathryn Beecroft
```

Here the main entry can be the heading for CILIP because the book emanates from CILIP and deals with CILIP's resources, members, etc.

It is *most important* to note that an exhibition catalogue can only be entered under the name of a corporate body if either

- the exhibition has a name itself, and is therefore treated as a corporate body (in which case it falls under (d) below); or
- the works in the exhibition consist *entirely* of material that belongs to a particular body, i.e. art gallery, museum, etc. A temporary exhibition of material which has simply been brought together at a particular gallery cannot be entered under the name of that gallery. In Fig. 5.8 (p. 99), therefore, we *cannot* use the heading for the Royal Academy as the main entry.

(c) those that record the collective thought of the body

21.1B2c

It is difficult to define exactly what is meant by 'collective thought', but the item *must* include some kind of expression of *opinion* or *recommendation*, not just be a statement of facts. There will usually be

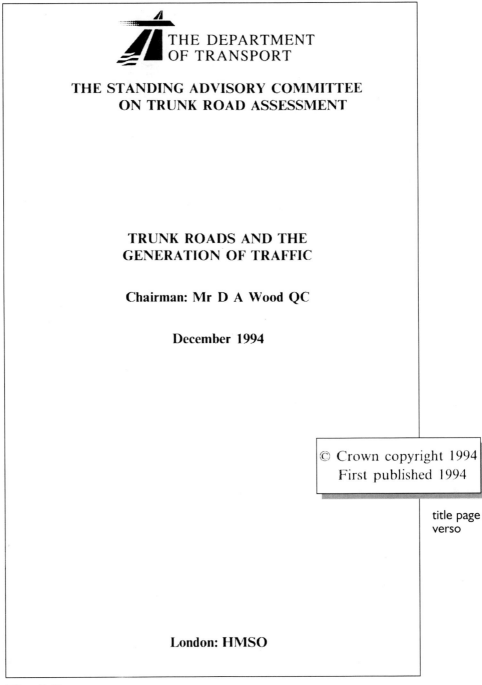

THE DEPARTMENT
OF TRANSPORT

**THE STANDING ADVISORY COMMITTEE
ON TRUNK ROAD ASSESSMENT**

**TRUNK ROADS AND THE
GENERATION OF TRAFFIC**

Chairman: Mr D A Wood QC

December 1994

© Crown copyright 1994
First published 1994

title page
verso

London: HMSO

Fig. 5.5

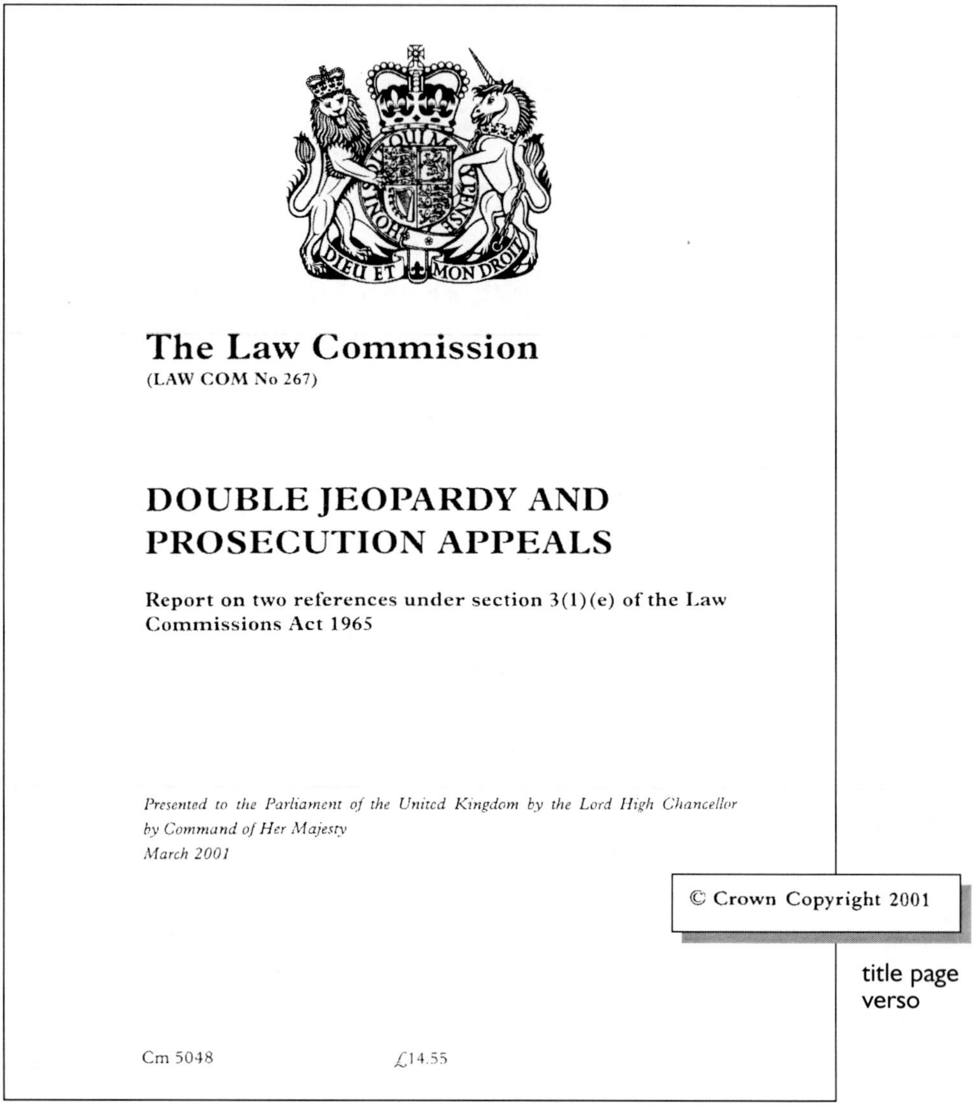

The Law Commission
(LAW COM No 267)

DOUBLE JEOPARDY AND PROSECUTION APPEALS

Report on two references under section 3(1)(e) of the Law Commissions Act 1965

Presented to the Parliament of the United Kingdom by the Lord High Chancellor by Command of Her Majesty
March 2001

© Crown Copyright 2001

title page verso

Cm 5048   £14.55

Fig. 5.6

recommendations, official statements of position, or policy statements. Royal Commissions and the like are good examples of this kind.

Examples
(Fig. 5.5, p. 95)

```
Trunk roads and the generation of traffic /
the Standing Advisory Committee on Trunk Road
Assessment ; chairman D.A. Wood
```

Main entry under the heading for the Standing Advisory Committee.

(Fig. 5.6, opposite)

```
Double jeopardy and prosecution appeals :
report on two references under section
3(1)(e) of the Law Commissions Act 1965
```

(rest of description omitted)

This clearly emanates from the Law Commission, as it has been caused to be published by the Commission, and it represents the judgement of the Commission.

(d) those that report the collective activity of a conference, etc. 21.1B2d
Note that

- the conference, etc., must fall within the definition of a corporate body; if it does not, this rule does not apply
- this in effect means that it must be named in the item.

It is not essential for the actual word 'conference' to appear; other synonyms are 'symposium', 'colloquium', 'round table', etc.

Examples
(Fig. 5.1, p. 89)

```
Proceedings of the Third International
Pineapple Symposium : Pattaya, Thailand, 12-
20 November 1998 / editors S. Subhadrabandhu,
P. Chairidchai
```

Main entry under the heading for the Symposium.

(Fig. 5.7, overleaf)

```
Sixteenth International Seaweed Symposium:
proceedings of the Sixteenth International
Seaweed Symposium, held in Cebu City,
Philippines, April 1998 / guest editors
Joanna M. Kain (Jones), Murray T. Brown &
Marc Lahaye
```

Main entry under the heading for the Symposium.

Before the AACR2 amendments of October 2001 the conference, etc., had to be *prominently* named in the item. This was very inconvenient, because quite often a book of conference proceedings might name the conference but not in one of the places in the book that count as 'prominently'. I mention this in case you find catalogue records which according to the present rule appear to be wrong. **0.8**

Hydrobiologia

The International Journal on Limnology and Marine Sciences

Volumes 398/399

Sixteenth International
Seaweed Symposium

*Proceedings of the Sixteenth
International Seaweed Symposium,
held in Cebu City, Philippines,
April 1998*

Guest Editors:
Joanna M. Kain (Jones),
Murray T. Brown &
Marc Lahaye

For Table of Contents see pp. ix–xiv

Published by Kluwer Academic Publishers, Spuiboulevard 50, P.O. Box 17, 3300 AA Dordrecht, The Netherlands, and 101 Philip Drive, Norwell, MA 02061, U.S.A.

title page
verso

Fig. 5.7

Sometimes it is difficult to tell whether the book actually represents the papers of the conference, or whether it is more loosely based on them. If you are in doubt, treat it as though it does not, and do not apply this rule. You can make an *added entry* for the name of the conference if necessary.

Sometimes a book may contain the proceedings of two or more conferences. In this case you will make the main entry for the first, and added entries for the others, assuming that not more than three are included in all.

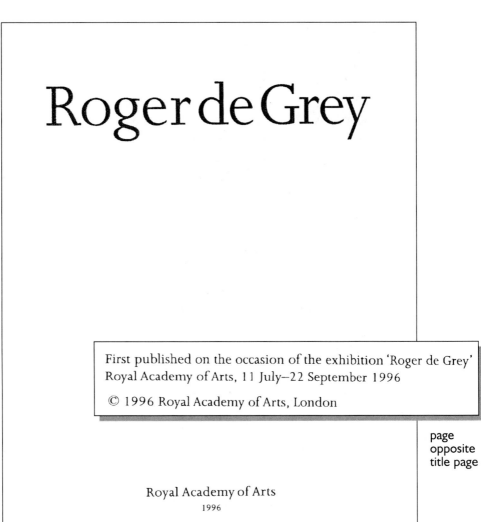

Fig. 5.8

An individual conference paper, published separately, would never fall under this rule. You would have to catalogue it as a separate work, and the main entry would be its author.

Exhibitions   21.1B2d

It is very seldom that this rule is applied in relation to exhibitions, simply because it is very rare for an exhibition to have an explicit name. You cannot infer from the title of the catalogue that the exhibition has the same name. The commonest occurrence is for very well-known historic exhibitions such as the Great Exhibition of 1851.

There is a considerable body of opinion *against* taking an exhibition to have a name even if it appears to be explicitly stated. Fig. 5.8 (p. 99), for example, refers to 'the exhibition "Roger de Grey"', but it is highly unlikely that most art librarians would wish to see this treated as a named exhibition. This is a difficult area, and more clarification would be desirable. For further guidance see the Arlis guidelines (Arlis 2000).

Whenever you think that the item you are cataloguing might fall under rule **21.1B2**, you *must* read through the subsections of the rule very carefully to establish whether it really does. If you cannot say categorically that it does come under one of these rules then it cannot be entered under a corporate body.

Sometimes an item is produced by a nameless subordinate part of a body which has a name. Because the body responsible for the production does not have a name, it cannot be used as the main entry, and neither can the main body, even though that has a name.

Example
(Fig. 4.17, p. 76)

```
Congestion charging : London Assembly
scrutiny report. - London : Greater London
Authority, 2000
```

Although this has been published by the Greater London Authority it is the work of an unnamed Panel. Main entry under title.

Items with both corporate body and personal author

Even when you have established that the item falls under rule **21.1B2** there still remains a problem: which has precedence, personal authorship, or entry under corporate body? Nothing is specifically stated in the rules, which is very unsatisfactory and confusing. What happens if the item falls under rule **21.1B2** but also appears to have a personal author? The rules tell us nothing *in themselves*, but the answer becomes apparent when you start to look at the examples which follow. **21.1A, 21.1B**

From these it becomes obvious that *entry under corporate body*, if it applies, *takes precedence over personal authorship*. This means that, for example, a catalogue of a collection in a particular museum, provided that it emanates from the museum, will be entered under the heading for the museum even *if it has a personal author*. **21.4A, 21.4B**

Pre-Raphaelite Drawings
in the British Museum

J. A. Gere

© 1994 Trustees of the British Museum

Published by British Museum Press
A division of British Museum Publications Ltd
46 Bloomsbury Street
London WC1B 3QQ

title page
verso

Published for the
Trustees of the British Museum
by British Museum Press

Fig. 5.9

Example
(Fig. 5.9, above)

```
Pre-Raphaelite drawings in the British Museum
/ J.A. Gere
```

Here the catalogue emanates from the British Museum and is entirely devoted to material which forms part of its collections. It is therefore entered under the heading for the Museum, even though it also has a personal author.

It follows from this that you must always have entry under corporate body in your mind before deciding to enter an item under a personal author. In most cases, however, it is immediately obvious that it does not apply, and you need not consider it further.

The other *most important point* is that you must not enter an item under a corporate body if it does not fall into any of the categories listed. This is a common mistake to make, and you can only avoid it if you read the rule very carefully and consider whether it *really* applies. If you do not keep this clearly in mind, you will be tempted to enter all kinds of things under the name of a corporate body simply because you cannot find anything else.

21.1B2 a–f

Before this rule was invented, it was common to enter all kinds of publications under the name of the organization that published them, simply because they were the publisher and there was no other obvious name to use. Most of these would *not* now come under this rule, and if they have no personal author the main entry will be title.

It is impossible in a book such as this to give enough examples for you to gain the appropriate experience, especially as you need to see the whole item, not just the title page. You should get an experienced and knowledgeable cataloguer to discuss as wide a range of real examples with you as possible.

Here is an example of an item which would *not* be entered under the name of a corporate body:

Example
(Fig. 5.10, opposite)

```
Winward Fearon on collateral warranties /
David L. Cornes, Richard Winward
```

Here Winward Fearon is the name of a firm, so it is a corporate body. Although published by Blackwell, we can probably assume that the book *emanates* from Winward Fearon, because they have 'caused it to be published'. However, it does *not* fall under any of the subrules here, and so it cannot have its main entry under the heading for Winward Fearon.

21.1B2 a–f

Title entry

21.1C

If an item is not entered either under a personal author or under a corporate body, the only thing that remains is the title, and this is provided for briefly. It is amplified later.

We have now seen the basic rules. The rest of the chapter goes into

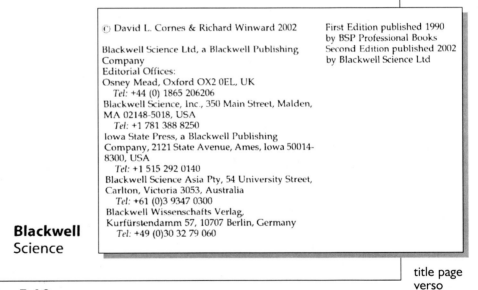

Winward Fearon
on
Collateral Warranties

SECOND EDITION

David L Cornes
BSc(Eng), AKC, FICE, CEng, FCIArb

Solicitor of the Supreme Court
Partner, Winward Fearon

Richard Winward
LLB, FCIArb, F.Inst.CES

Solicitor of the Supreme Court
Partner, Winward Fearon

© David L. Cornes & Richard Winward 2002

Blackwell Science Ltd, a Blackwell Publishing
Company
Editorial Offices:
Osney Mead, Oxford OX2 0EL, UK
  Tel: +44 (0) 1865 206206
Blackwell Science, Inc., 350 Main Street, Malden,
MA 02148-5018, USA
  Tel: +1 781 388 8250
Iowa State Press, a Blackwell Publishing
Company, 2121 State Avenue, Ames, Iowa 50014-
8300, USA
  Tel: +1 515 292 0140
Blackwell Science Asia Pty, 54 University Street,
Carlton, Victoria 3053, Australia
  Tel: +61 (0)3 9347 0300
Blackwell Wissenschafts Verlag,
Kurfürstendamm 57, 10707 Berlin, Germany
  Tel: +49 (0)30 32 79 060

First Edition published 1990
by BSP Professional Books
Second Edition published 2002
by Blackwell Science Ltd

Blackwell
Science

title page
verso

Fig. 5.10

more detail on specific cases, but before we look at those let us just have a reminder, that:

> Whatever the kind of item, the only possible main entry is one of the following:
>
> - corporate body
> - personal author
> - title.
>
> There are no other possibilities.

We can now look at some of the more detailed rules.

Changes of persons or bodies responsible for a work   21.3

This rule is seldom used, but you should remember that it is here. It is especially useful when you have a multipart work and the authors change from one volume to another. The problem, of course, can be deciding whether you have a multipart work!   21.3A2

    Rule **21.4** simply illustrates a large number of examples of the application of rule **21.1**, for both personal authors and corporate bodies. It is worth studying these examples carefully, particularly in relation to entry under corporate body.   21.4

Miscellaneous cases

The next group of rules is rather miscellaneous, and covers some unusual situations that seldom arise. They have nothing in common and it is not clear why they are lumped together in this way.

Works erroneously or fictitiously attributed to a person or corporate body   21.4C1

The examples given in AACR2 are the obvious ones: an author writes a work and pretends that it has been written by a fictional character. We all know that it hasn't really, and it seems natural to enter it under the name of the real author.

Example
(Fig. 10.2, p. 188)

```
The life and strange surprizing adventures of
Robinson Crusoe, of York, mariner : who lived
eight and twenty years … / written by himself ;
Daniel Defoe ; with an introduction by J.M.
Coetzee
```

Main entry under the heading for Defoe.

    Perhaps in this case the work is so well known that it would be better to omit 'written by himself' altogether.

It is difficult to think of an example where a corporate body would apply, and it is noteworthy that no example is given of this.   **21.4C2**

Works by heads of state, etc.   **21.4D**

This too is fairly unusual, but it applies to people like the President of the United States, or the Pope. Such people may write works in a private capacity or in their capacity as holder of the office. Depending on which it is, we may either use their personal name as the heading or construct a corporate name which indicates the office they hold. The actual form of this name is dealt with in AACR2 Chapter 24, because it is a kind of corporate body.   **24.18A**

The really unusual thing about this rule is that you have to make an *added entry* under the other form. This means that all such works will appear under *both* forms of name. This goes against the normal spirit of authority control, that you do not use two different forms of name for the same person, let alone make entries under two different forms of name. Normally you would make cross-references between the forms of name, rather than making duplicate entries.   **Type 9**

Works of unknown or uncertain authorship or by unnamed groups   **21.5**

If a work is of unknown or uncertain authorship, or if it emanates from a corporate body that has no name, it must be entered under title. This is pretty obvious, as there would be no alternative.   **21.5A**

More surprisingly, we enter anonymous items under the probable author if there is one. You are not likely to come across this very often.   **21.5B**

Some works, particularly 19th-century books, have *descriptive phrases* representing the author, rather than an actual name. These expressions can be used as access points *provided that the real name of the author is not known.* (We need to look at AACR2 Chapter 22, of course, to establish the *form of heading* to be used.) Remember that you may only use this rule if the authorship is not known, *not* for every author who has ever used such a phrase. This means that all the books written 'by the Author of Elizabeth and her German garden' would be entered under the author's actual name, because this is known, and this rule would not apply.   **21.5C**   **22.11D**

Works by more than one person or body

So far the rules have assumed that only one personal author or one corporate body was involved. But obviously many items, probably most, involve more than one person (and sometimes more than one body) in various ways.

Individuals may contribute to a work in all kinds of ways. In addition to personal authors, we may have

- an editor
- an illustrator
- a translator
- a reviser
- the writer of a preface

and other types of responsibility.

Writers of prefaces are not specifically mentioned in AACR2 and it is therefore not clear whether they would normally count as contributors.

AACR2 uses different terms to describe the different ways in which more than one person or body may contribute to a work. These terms are:

- shared responsibility
- mixed responsibility.

Neither term is self-explanatory. It is not particularly important to know which is which, but what *is* important is to be able to find the right rule, and for this purpose the correct terminology can be useful.

The essential difference is that

- shared responsibility means that all those involved have done the *same kind* of thing in contributing to the work; e.g. they have collaborated in writing a book, or they have contributed different chapters to it; whereas
- mixed responsibility means that those involved have done *different kinds of thing* to contribute to the work; e.g. someone may have written a book, which someone else has revised, or translated, or illustrated.

Clearly the two kinds of responsibility are not mutually exclusive, and it is common to have a work that is of both shared and mixed responsibility.

Shared responsibility · 21.6

The rule starts with a list of the possible cases of shared responsibility. The commonest of these is (a), works produced by the collaboration of two or more persons, i.e. what we would call 'joint authorship'. The rule is divided into two main sections:

- Principal responsibility indicated · 21.6B
- Principal responsibility not indicated · 21.6C

but in practice this seldom makes any difference to the result. It is very rare for there to be any indication of principal responsibility. What you normally have is a statement that two or three authors have written the book, with no indication that one of them is more important than the other(s).

You are *not* expected to examine the content of the item to establish whether one of the contributors has principal responsibility; you rely simply on 'the wording or the layout of the chief source of information'. This means that if the preface happens to say that the second-named author has in fact written almost all of the work, you ignore this unless it is also indicated in the chief source of information. **21.6B1**

We can summarize these rules by saying that

- if there is an indication that one of the contributors is principally responsible, this person should have the main entry, even if not named first **21.6B1**
- in other cases, the first named person has main entry. **21.6C1**

In either case, you make added entries for the other contributors provided that there are not more than another two (i.e. three altogether). **21.6B1, 21.6B2,**
People who know nothing about cataloguing are usually surprised **21.6C1** that it is not possible to enter an item under some kind of heading for *two names* at the same time. However, it is not. Each is a *separate* access point, leading individually to the description.

Some OPACs allow you to type authors' names in more than one box, and thus retrieve items with two authors without knowing the title.
Very exceptionally, and unexemplified in AACR2, a form of name has been used for two people who work very closely together and do not produce anything separately, such as the sculptors Gilbert & George. In these cases the name is treated as being like that of a corporate body.

Example
(Fig. 4.2, p. 28)

```
The natural history of moles / Martyn L.
Gorman and R. David Stone
```

Main entry under the heading for Gorman. Added entry under the heading for Stone. There is nothing to show that one person is chiefly responsible, so we simply take the names in the order in which they appear.

More than three contributors

When we get to *more than three* contributors a different rule applies. You will remember (pp. 49–50) that in copying out the statement of responsibility in the description you had to stop when you reached more than three names in any one statement, and this rule corresponds with that. Because in those cases you are not allowed to mention more than the first named contributor you clearly cannot make entries for them. (You must *never* make entries for anything or anyone not mentioned in the description.) **21.6C2 1.1F5**

21.29F

Only the first named person is mentioned in the description, and it is only this person who can get an access point, and this is as an *added entry* only. In this situation the contribution of one person is not thought significant enough to warrant main entry, which is therefore under *title*. **21.6C2**

Example

(Fig. 4.13, p. 47)

```
Bird census techniques / Colin J. Bibby … [et
al.] ; illustrated by Sandra Lambton, RSPB
and Simon Mustoe
```

Main entry under title. Added entry under the heading for Bibby. You may also make added entries for Lambton, RSPB and Mustoe if you think them important. **21.30K2c**

Although I have used personal authors as examples, this rule applies equally (though much less commonly) to items entered under corporate body, where more than one is involved.

We can summarize so far:

one author:	main entry under author
two authors:	main entry under first author
	added entry under second author
three authors:	main entry under first author
	added entry under second author
	added entry under third author
more than three authors:	main entry under title
	added entry under first author

Shared pseudonyms 21.6D

If two or more people collaborate and use a single pseudonym, you use this as the heading. In reality, if you did not know that a pseudonym represented two people you would not be able to do other than what the rule suggests. In practice you seldom see this kind of thing.

Collections of works by different persons or bodies 21.7

Very often a publication consists of contributions by several different people or bodies. The commonest occurrence of this is where you have an edited work, with chapters all written by different people.

Just as when there were more than three authors we had to enter the item under its title, we do that here too, in most cases. It is not quite as simple as this because the rule is divided into two parts:

- With collective title 21.7B
- Without collective title 21.7C

'Collective title' in this case simply means an overall title for the whole volume, as opposed to the titles of the individual pieces within it. It is clearly much commoner for an item to have a collective title.

With collective title 21.7B1

In this case the main entry has to be the title. Make added entries for up to three editors or compilers if they are named prominently. If there are more, you can make an added entry for the first only (and of course this is the only one that will have been included in the description).

Example
(Fig. 5.3, p. 91)

```
Advanced polymer composites for structural
applications in construction : proceedings of
the first international conference, held at
Southampton University, UK, on 15-17 April
2002 / edited by R.A. Shenoi, S.S.J. Moy,
L.C. Holloway
```

Main entry under title. Added entry under the heading for Shenoi. Added entry under the heading for Moy. Added entry under the heading for Holloway.

If the item contains either two or three named works you make name-title added entries for them (see p. 112). 21.7B1

Without collective title 21.7C1

In this case you enter it as if it contained the first work only, i.e. under the heading for that one. Make name-title added entries for other items. This is much less common.

Summary for collections

If no collective title:	first author
Collective title, up to three editors:	main entry under title, added entry for each editor
Collective title, more than three editors:	main entry under title, added entry for first editor

Works of mixed responsibility 21.8

The next portion of AACR2 Chapter 21 is taken up with works of 'mixed responsibility', which means items where different persons or bodies have made *different kinds* of contribution.

This major section is divided into two:

- works that are modifications of other works 21.9–
- mixed responsibility in new works 21.23

21.24–
21.27

each of which has a large number of rules. We shall look at the most commonly used ones.

The general rule is that works that are modifications of other works 21.9
are entered under heading appropriate to the *new work* if the modification has 'substantially changed the nature and content of the original 21.9A
or if the medium of expression has been changed'. It is easier to understand what this means when we look at the individual rules.

Adaptations 21.10

Adaptations of texts are entered under the heading for the adapter; this includes dramatizations, simplified versions for children or non-native speakers, etc.

Example

(Fig. 5.11, opposite)

```
Great expectations / Charles Dickens ; retold
by Florence Bell. - Oxford : Heinemann ELT,
1993. - 95 p. : ill. ; 20 cm. - (Heinemann
ELT guided readers. Upper level)
```

Here, although on the title page Dickens appears to be primarily

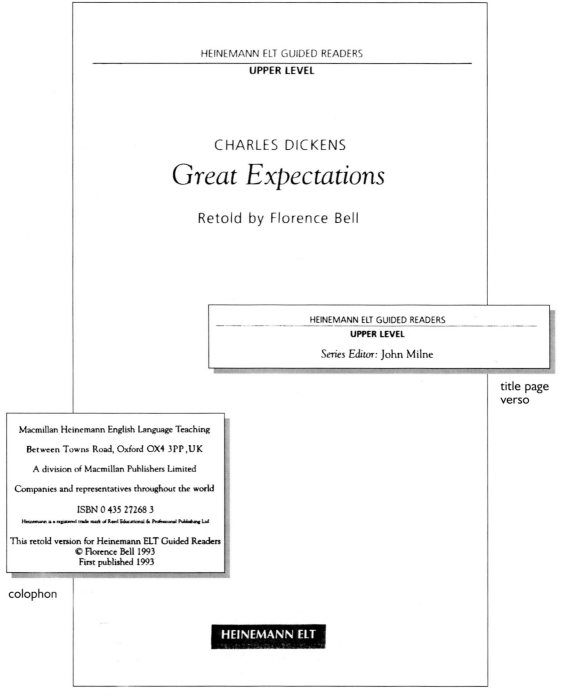

HEINEMANN ELT GUIDED READERS
UPPER LEVEL

CHARLES DICKENS
Great Expectations

Retold by Florence Bell

HEINEMANN ELT GUIDED READERS
UPPER LEVEL
Series Editor: John Milne

title page
verso

Macmillan Heinemann English Language Teaching

Between Towns Road, Oxford OX4 3PP ,UK

A division of Macmillan Publishers Limited

Companies and representatives throughout the world

ISBN 0 435 27268 3

Heinemann is a registered trade mark of Reed Educational & Professional Publishing Ltd

This retold version for Heinemann ELT Guided Readers
© Florence Bell 1993
First published 1993

colophon

HEINEMANN ELT

Fig. 5.11

responsible, the main entry will be under the heading for Bell, because she has rewritten the work.

Make a name-title added entry under the heading for Dickens. This means that having established what the form of heading for Dickens is, you will add the title *Great expectations* to it.

Illustrated texts   21.11A1
Illustrated texts are entered under the heading for the text (but note that *this is for pre-existing texts*; not for works of collaboration, which come later).

An exception is that if the illustrations are published separately they naturally   21.11B1
have to be catalogued as a work in their own right, which means that the illustrator is the main entry.

Revisions of texts   21.12
Often a work is revised by a different person, sometimes long after the original author is dead. Yet it may continue to bear the name of the original author, sometimes as part of the title. How should you enter this kind of work: under the original author or under the person who has revised it?

It would be very tedious if you had to answer this by looking at the actual text and comparing the editions word by word to see who had written what. The rule is therefore designed to avoid this by giving you a rule of thumb based *solely* on how the information is presented in the chief source of information.

There are two possibilities:

- original author considered responsible   21.12A1
- original author no longer considered responsible.   21.12B1

Original author considered responsible   21.12A1
The original author is considered for cataloguing purposes still to be responsible if either

- the original author is named in a statement of responsibility; or
- the original author is named in the title proper and no other person is named in a statement of responsibility or other title information.

In either of these cases you make the main entry under the name of the original author. Make an added entry for the reviser.

Example
(Fig. 5.12, opposite)

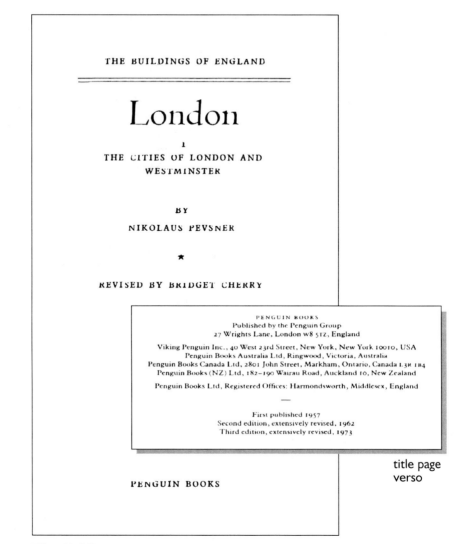

THE BUILDINGS OF ENGLAND

London

1

THE CITIES OF LONDON AND
WESTMINSTER

BY

NIKOLAUS PEVSNER

★

REVISED BY BRIDGET CHERRY

PENGUIN BOOKS
Published by the Penguin Group
27 Wrights Lane, London W8 5TZ, England

Viking Penguin Inc., 40 West 23rd Street, New York, New York 10010, USA
Penguin Books Australia Ltd, Ringwood, Victoria, Australia
Penguin Books Canada Ltd, 2801 John Street, Markham, Ontario, Canada L3R 1B4
Penguin Books (NZ) Ltd, 182–190 Wairau Road, Auckland 10, New Zealand

Penguin Books Ltd, Registered Offices: Harmondsworth, Middlesex, England

—

First published 1957
Second edition, extensively revised, 1962
Third edition, extensively revised, 1973

title page
verso

PENGUIN BOOKS

Fig. 5.12

```
London. 1, The cities of London and
Westminster / by Nikolaus Pevsner. - 3rd ed.
/ revised by Bridget Cherry
```

(See Chapter 6 of this book for the problems of multipart works.) The important point here is that Pevsner is still named in the statement of responsibility, and that there is a second statement relating to the revised edition.

If there is no original author, but only an editor, then of course this does not apply and you will have to enter it under title.

The rule is not helped by the ambiguity over the meaning of 'statement of responsibility' in AACR2. We have already seen that a statement of responsibility can be *included* (in the possessive case) in a title proper, whereas *this* rule seems to have to be interpreted as meaning that the statement of responsibility must be *separate* from the title proper. **1.1B2**

Original author no longer considered responsible **21.12B1**

The original author is considered no longer to be responsible *whenever rule 21.12A1 does not apply*. This is why this rule is phrased rather less precisely than the former, and gives an example only, rather than an exact specification.

The example is when the original author is named *only* in the title proper (not in any statement of responsibility) and some other person is named in the statement of responsibility or in a statement of responsibility relating to the edition.

In any such cases you treat the work as being a new work by the reviser and make the reviser the main entry. You make an added entry (name-title) under the heading for the original author.

Example

(Fig. 4.16, p. 55)

```
Winfield and Jolowicz on tort. - 14th ed. /
by W.V.H. Rogers
```

Here Winfield and Jolowicz are not named in a statement of responsibility, and the main entry must therefore be under the heading for Rogers.

Make name-title added entries for both Winfield and Jolowicz. This will involve finding out their correct names, and attaching the title proper of the original edition to the end of the headings.

As the original author is often represented only by a surname in the title it can sometimes take some research to find out the form of name required for the heading.

You cannot be expected to memorize this pair of rules. All you need to do is remember that they are there, and read them *very carefully* when you need to. The exact form of wording on the title page is paramount, and this is what will determine the main entry. **21.12A, 21.12B**

Notice that in all cases you make an added entry for whichever person does not get the main entry.

Texts published with commentary 21.13

Some kinds of work are often published with a commentary by a different person. The main types of material are probably

- editions of literary or philosophical texts
- editions of individual Acts of Parliament or their equivalent, either of which may have a commentary.

Note that for this rule to apply the item *must* contain *both* the text *and* the commentary. If it contains the commentary *only*, you treat that as a work in its own right.

Again it is the presentation of the chief source of information that determines whether the original or the commentary is regarded as the predominant feature.

If the commentary is emphasized, enter the item under the heading **21.13B1** for the person(s) who wrote the commentary.

If the text itself is emphasized, enter the item under the heading **21.13C1** appropriate for the text.

If the chief source of information is ambiguous see the special rule. **21.13D1**

Notice that, as in the case of revised editions, it is purely the chief source of information which counts in making the decision: you are *not* expected to look through the item itself and try to assess the relative contributions of the persons or organizations involved.

It is quite normal for a commentary on an individual Act of Parliament to include the complete text of that Act. If it is presented on the title page as being a commentary on the Act then you will enter it under the name of the commentator. But you could have an identical book which happens to be presented as the text of the Act, accompanied by a commentary, and in that case you would treat it as an edition of the text of the Act.

Although this may seem illogical, the rule is designed to save you work.

Example
(Fig. 5.13, overleaf)

```
The Freedom of Information Act 2000 / Michael
Supperstone, Timothy Pitt-Payne. - London :
Butterworths, 2001. - xii, 176 p. ; 24 cm. -
(Butterworths new law guides). - Includes the
text of the Act
```

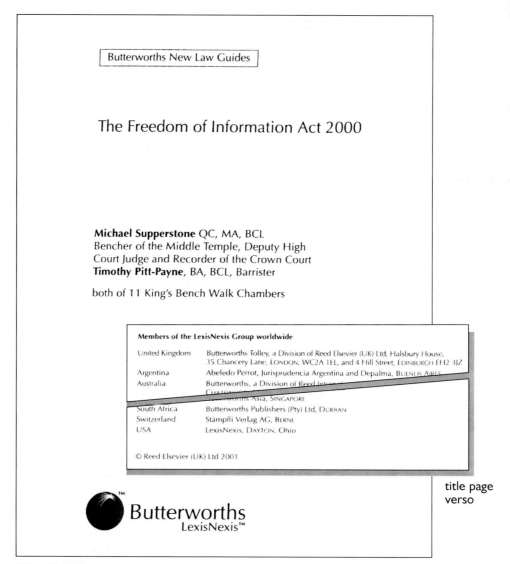

Fig. 5.13

(Notice the capitalization of the name of the Act.)   A.20A

This commentary includes the complete text of the Act, and so this fact is mentioned in the Note area. However, the title page presents the book as being a book *about* the Act *by* Supperstone and Pitt-Payne. Main entry is therefore under the heading for Supperstone, with added entry for Pitt-Payne, and a name-title added entry for the heading for the Act.

Translations   21.14

Translations are different from adaptations, in that they are regarded as being just the original text in a different language. This means that

the original author is given the main entry. Rules about added entries **21.30K1**
for the translator are quite detailed, but, as we shall see, there is a good
deal of flexibility in applying them (see p. 125).

Example
(Fig. 10.1, p. 186)

```
The coming of the book : the impact of
printing 1450-1800 / Lucien Febvre, Henri-
Jean Martin ; translated by David Gerard ;
edited by Geoffrey Nowell-Smith and David
Wootton. - London : Verso, 1984. - 378 p. ;
21 cm. - Translation of: L'apparition du
livre. - English ed. originally published:
London : NLB, 1976
```

Main entry under the heading for Febvre. Added entry under the
heading for Martin. Possible added entry under the heading for Ger-
ard. Probable added entries under the headings for Nowell-Smith and
Wootton.

Texts published with biographical/critical material **21.15**
This little-used rule deals with cases where there is a mixture of material by
and about a person. Again you rely on the way the chief source of information is presented.

Art works **21.16–**
Don't be misled by the heading. Remember that we are still in a main **21.17**
section on *mixed responsibility*. This is *not* a general rule telling you everything you want to know about art works; it is only about those which
are of mixed responsibility.

Adaptations of art works **21.16**
This is divided into two sections:

- adaptations from one medium of the graphic arts to another
- reproductions of art works of any medium.

The distinction can be confusing, but if you think about it it all makes
sense. The first refers to two-dimensional works and the fact that they may be **21.16A**
'adapted' by being copied by a different artist. These are therefore similar to
the literary adaptations which we saw earlier (pp. 110–12) and are treated in
the same way. This means that the main entry is the heading for the adapter,
and if the name of the adapter is not known, the main entry is the title.
Beware of entering such works under the original artist.
    A reproduction of the second type implies a *mechanical* copy, such as a photo- **21.16B**

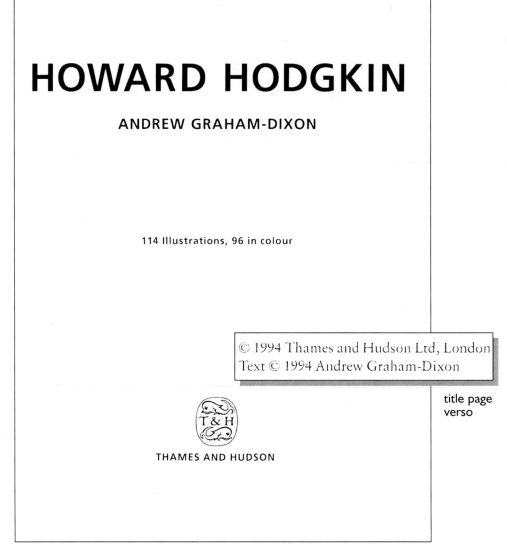

HOWARD HODGKIN

ANDREW GRAHAM-DIXON

114 Illustrations, 96 in colour

© 1994 Thames and Hudson Ltd, London
Text © 1994 Andrew Graham-Dixon

THAMES AND HUDSON

title page
verso

Fig. 5.14

graph. In this case there has clearly been no *new* artistic effort, and these are treated as if they were the same as the original and entered accordingly.

Reproductions of two or more art works 21.17
This rule is used rather more often. Notice that it only applies to *two or more* works; single works have been covered already. Again it is divided in two:

- Without text 21.17A
- With text. 21.17B

This distinction has some rather strange results.

Without text 21.17A1

In this case, the item will be entered under the name of the artist. If there is more than one artist, obviously you need to look at the general rules about *shared responsibility* also, which we have already seen (pp. 106–8).

With text 21.17B1

In this case it is the writer of the text who is the main entry *if* that person 'is represented as author in the chief source of information'. This means 'if the writer's name is presented in the way in which an author's name would be presented in an ordinary book', i.e. it does *not* say 'edited by', or anything else that would imply that the named person is something other than an author.

The result of this is that you can have a book of reproductions of an artist's pictures, with a very slight introductory text, and provided that the title page is presented in such a way that the *writer* appears to be the author of the book then the *writer* will have the main entry. In all other respects the book might be exactly the same as another one that has the same amount of introductory text but without anyone's name being given on the title page.

This is therefore another of these rules which are designed to help you, the cataloguer, to decide what to do, without having to examine the item in detail.

You do of course make an added entry under the name of the artist.

Example

(Fig. 5.14, opposite)

```
Howard Hodgkin / Andrew Graham-Dixon. -
London : Thames and Hudson, 1994. - 192 p. :
114 ill. (96 col.) ; 27 cm.
```

Main entry under the heading for Graham-Dixon. Added entry under the heading for Hodgkin.

If no one is represented as the author, enter the item under the heading for the artist. This is what you would do with Fig. 5.8 (p. 99). 21.17B1

Mixed responsibility in musical works and sound recordings

21.18–21.23

It is beyond the scope of this book to go into enough detail to deal adequately with music or sound recordings, but these are the rules that you need to consult.

Mixed responsibility in new works

21.24–21.27

We now move on to a new section, which deals with contributors making different kinds of contribution to new works, as opposed to making changes to existing ones. In practice, although this is a different set of rules it seldom results in a different main entry.

Collaboration between artist and writer

21.24

This refers to items that are produced by a writer and an artist *jointly*. You simply enter such items under whichever person is named *first*, *unless* there is some indication that the other is more important; as usual, this has to be in the wording or layout of the chief source of information. This is therefore in line with other rules that we have seen, that the first person named has the main entry unless there is good reason to do something else.

The commonest applications of this rule are to natural history books, particularly field guides, where the illustrations are usually regarded as integral to the text, and to books of photographs.

Example

(Fig. 4.7, p. 37)

```
Riches of the wild : land mammals of south-
east Asia / Earl of Cranbrook ; with coloured
plates by A.M. Hughes
```

This is an example of the more normal situation, where the illustrations are subordinate. Main entry under the heading for the Earl of Cranbrook. Added entry (discretionary) under the heading for Hughes.

Reports of interviews and exchanges

21.25

This rule is comparable to others in that it is the person who is chiefly responsible for the content that is given the main entry. You therefore need to establish whose words constitute most of the item, and for once this involves doing more than just looking at the chief source of information.

The rule is comparatively seldom needed, but is of course useful when dealing with sound recordings and videorecordings, when you may be cataloguing the recording of a discussion.

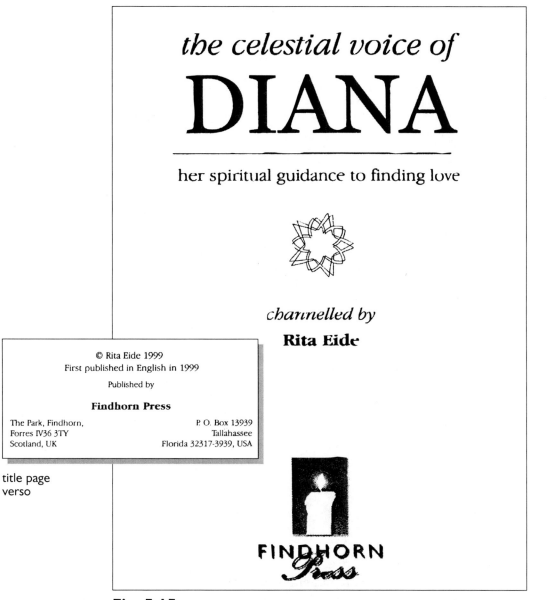

the celestial voice of

DIANA

her spiritual guidance to finding love

channelled by

Rita Eide

© Rita Eide 1999
First published in English in 1999

Published by

Findhorn Press

The Park, Findhorn,   P. O. Box 13939
Forres IV36 3TY   Tallahassee
Scotland, UK   Florida 32317-3939, USA

title page
verso

FINDHORN *Press*

Fig. 5.15

Spirit communications

21.26

This usually causes surprise and raises a laugh. If a medium receives some work from a dead person and has it published, the work will be entered under the heading for the spirit of the dead person, *not* under the name of the medium.

Example
(Fig. 5.15, p. 121)

```
The celestial voice of Diana : her spiritual
guidance to finding love / channelled by Rita
Eide
```

Diana, Princess of Wales, has been active since her death and has produced at least two books so far. Main entry here under the heading for her spirit, with added entry for the medium.

Note that the heading used is for the spirit (the form of heading is discussed in AACR2 Chapter 22), not for the actual person. This will therefore differentiate the items by the spirit from those by the living person, so that they are not under the same heading.

   In all cases you make an added entry for the medium.

Academic disputations
If you ever have cause to apply this rule please write and tell me.

Summary for mixed responsibility	
Adaptations:	main entry under adapter
Revisions:	(see rules)
Commentaries:	main entry under commentator
Translations:	main entry under original
Collaboration of artist and writer:	main entry under first named *unless* another given prominence

Related works
This rule is simply here as a reminder that when you are cataloguing you treat each item as an individual piece, and the fact that it is related to some other work does not determine its main entry. The list of examples will give you an idea of the kinds of thing that are meant.

   For example, if someone compiles an index to Dickens's works, it is treated as a work in its own right, and not catalogued as if it were by Dickens himself. Similarly, if someone writes a commentary on a literary text and publishes it *without* the text itself, it will be catalogued as being a work by the writer of the commentary, not as an edition of the text.

   The only reason you need to be aware of the relationship to another

22.14

21.27

21.12

21.28

21.28A1

work is so that you can make an *added entry*. This will enable catalogue users who might expect it to be catalogued under the related work to find it more easily.

Special rules

21.31–
21.39

It seems to make more sense to look at the special rules now, and to leave added entries, which in AACR2 come at this point, till later.

We will not look at all of the special rules, because most of them never arise, but I will pick out a few of the more commonly needed ones.

Laws, etc.

21.31

Even a non-legal collection is likely to have copies of one or two individual laws, and so you ought to know how these should be catalogued. This rule does not give the whole story, however, because to look at it fully we need to consider uniform titles as well; these are covered in AACR2 Chapter 25. At this stage we are only considering the 25.15 main entry, which in most cases is the name of the jurisdiction. We shall have to wait till later (pp. 168–9) to find out how to construct the heading.

The main thing to note is that laws can be local as well as national, which means that the main entry may be the heading for a city or a state, not just a country, as you might expect.

Notice that Bills go under the heading for the *legislative body*, rather 21.31B3 than the heading for the jurisdiction. This makes them different from actual Acts.

Sacred scriptures

21.37

Because these have no definable author they have to be entered under title. Again we shall need to look at AACR2 Chapter 25 (Chapter 10 of 25.17–
25.18 this book) for the rules on uniform titles, which are usually applied here.

Added entries

21.29–
21.30

This section brings together all the references to added entries that we have already seen, and also goes into further detail regarding some of them.

You will notice that there is rather more flexibility about added entries than there is about the question of deciding which is the main entry. For example:

- You are allowed to make an added entry under a heading 'if some cat- 21.29C alogue users might suppose that the description of the item would be found under that heading ...'. It is always difficult to imagine what catalogue users might suppose, but this allows for some added entries that might not otherwise be permitted.

- You are allowed to make an added entry if 'in the context of a given catalogue' it is required. This might allow you to make an added entry for a person whom you consider to be important for your collection but who would not otherwise get one under the general rules. **21.29D**

What is especially important is that *all* added entries must be justifiable and comprehensible in terms of what appears in the description. You *must not* make added entries for any person, body or title that has not been mentioned in the description. This means that you will occasionally have to add a Note area in order to explain an added entry that you want to make. **21.29F**

MARC: Added entry tags are: 700 for persons, 710 for corporate bodies, 711 for conferences

Specific rules for added entries **21.30**

Rules **21.30A–E** really just summarize the rules for added entries that we have already seen in going through Chapter 21. The rest of this section (rules **21.30F–M**) deals with the more special cases. You do not need to worry much about this, because, as I mentioned above, there is a great deal of flexibility in assigning added entries anyway.

Note the following specific rules:

Other related persons or bodies **21.30F1**

If a volume of essays is dedicated to a particular person (i.e. it is a Festschrift) you should make an added entry for that person.

Example
(Fig. 5.2, p. 90)

```
Homotopy theory and its applications : a
conference on algebraic topology in honor of
Samuel Gitler, August 9-13 1993, Cocoyoc,
Mexico ; Alejandro Adem, R. James Milgram,
Douglas C. Ravenel, editors. - Providence,
R.I. : American Mathematical Society, 1995
```

Main entry under title. Added entries under the headings for Adem, Milgram and Ravenel. Added entry under the heading for Gitler. Added entry under the heading for the American Mathematical Society. It is normal to make such added entries for names of non-commercial publishers. **21.30E1**

Make an added entry for the museum where an exhibition was held. **21.30F1**
You would do this for Fig. 5.8 (p. 99).

Other relationships
21.30H1

This rule allows you to make an added entry under any other heading that would be useful, and therefore allows great flexibility.

Notice, however, that it specifically forbids you to make an added entry for a person or body who is merely the *subject* of an item. In practice you would probably make such an entry, but it would be a *subject* added entry, and, as such, nothing to do with AACR2, which does not deal with subject retrieval in any way.

MARC:
245 first indicator 1 is designed to generate an added entry; second indicator specifies number of characters to be ignored in filing.
246 field is used for variant titles. See a detailed manual for explanation of indicators.

Titles
21.30J1

There is an assumption that most items will need a title added entry if the title is not the main entry. Most computerized systems will take care of this automatically without you having to do anything.

You may, however, need to make an added entry separately for a variant form of the title, or, as in the case of *Eileen Ford's a more beautiful you in twenty-one days*, for the part of the title following the personal name.

Special rules on added entries in certain cases
21.30K

This rule deals with translators and illustrators. Although considerable detail is given, in most cases whether you make an added entry will depend mostly on how important you feel the translator or illustrator is and how important you think that access point would be to your users.

Series
21.30L1

The question of when to make an added entry for a series statement is one which beginners usually find very difficult. We have already looked at the description aspect of series statements, and I mentioned that there are two different MARC tags for them. The reason for the different tags is to do with whether you want an added entry under the series name or not.

The two MARC tags are:

MARC:
440 second indicator is filing indicator

- 440 which produces an added entry; and
- 490 which does not produce an added entry.

(Of course, whether they *actually* produce an added entry or not depends on how your automated system is set up, but this is the idea behind it.)

You may be wondering why you would want an added entry for a series at all. Series statements vary in usefulness and meaning, and there is therefore scope for discretion in deciding whether to have an added entry or not.

Generally speaking, if the series statement has some distinct meaning and says something useful, it is worth making an added entry for it, and in this case you will use field 440.

On the other hand, if the series statement is of the kind:

'Research paper' or
'Works' or
'A Penguin original'

it is usually regarded as not being very useful for access purposes, and it would be coded as 490.

Like so much else in cataloguing it is of course often a matter of discretion and judgement whether an added entry is needed or not. In an ideal situation you would include series statements in your authority control system (see Chapter 9 of this book), so that a record of your policy is maintained.

Another thing that your authority file should record is whether you wish to include the *number* as part of an added entry. In AACR2 this is optional. Some series are better understood when viewed in numerical order, while for others it does not matter at all. **21.30L1**

Some libraries have arbitrarily decided that certain types of series statement should automatically be coded as 490 so as not to generate added entries. The British Library did this some years ago for series that include the name of the publisher.

MARC:
490 first
indicator 1
shows presence
of added entry.

What adds to the beginner's confusion is that it is quite possible to code a series statement as 490 but then to provide an added entry separately using an 830 field. Why would you want to do this?

The answer is that you would want to do it when the series statement *as it stands* is not 'in added entry form', by which we mean that it is not in a suitable structure to be used as an access point, but if rearranged it could be made useful.

It is easiest to understand this by returning to a specific example:

Example
(Fig. 4.11, p. 43)

(Volume four of a history of Cheshire)

You will remember (pp. 78–9) that because this is all connected together you must copy it as it appears. But no one would want to look this up under such a topsy-turvy form, and you therefore need to create an added entry the 'right' way round:

```
A history of Cheshire ; v. 4
```

which would be the more normal form. The provision of 490 and 830 fields allows you do this, as follows:

```
490 1_$aVolume four of a history of Cheshire
830 _2$aA history of Cheshire ; $vv. 4
```

6 Multipart works

Considering how common they are, AACR2's treatment of multipart works is deplorable and quite inadequate. In this chapter I will look first at the problems of description, and will then conclude with a short section on access points.

Description

Throughout this discussion I use the term 'multipart title' to mean the title that applies to *all* the parts, and 'part number' and 'part title' to refer to the number and title of the individual part. In the case of books we would usually use the term 'volume' for 'part'.

Two possible models are provided:

MARC: 245:
use $n for part
number,
$p for part title.

1 Part number and/or part title included in Title and statement of responsibility area   1.1B9, 1.1C2

```
Multipart title. Part number [GMD] /
statement of responsibility [etc.]
```

This could presumably be extended to include the part title also (or instead of the part number), and it appears from elsewhere that the punctuation to introduce the part title is 'comma space', and that the part title must have a capital letter.   A.4D1

This model is also implied by the rules about uniform titles for parts of a work, where examples of cross-references are given in the same form.   25.6

MARC 21 cannot
deal with this
system.

2 Part number and/or part title moved to separate area   13.6

```
Multipart title [GMD] / statement of
responsibility [etc., followed by the rest of
the description]

        Part number: Part title
```

i.e., the description of the individual part is relegated to a separate area of the description which is not otherwise used. The whole description of the multipart title comes first.

Notice that in this system the part title is introduced by 'colon space' rather than 'comma space'.

The second system appears only under the heading 'Multilevel description' in AACR2 Chapter 13, which otherwise deals with analytical entries. It has the advantage of being infinitely extensible, in cases where the parts are further divided. It is also easier to place edition statements and statements of responsibility correctly so that they appear with the title to which they refer.

The implication is that the latter rule would not normally be used.

You are therefore recommended to use the first system. There is another problem, however. In the Title and statement of responsibility there is *no* provision

- to abbreviate words like 'Volume' or 'Part'   **B.4A**
- to convert roman numerals or numbers written as words into arabic numerals.   **C.2B1**

This accounts for the example

     1.1B9

```
Faust. Part one
```

in AACR2.

Conventionally these rules are broken, and such abbreviations and changes *are* made, to assist filing and arrangement. It is high time that this problem was looked at and resolved.

Multipart works and series

One of the difficulties that beginners have is in deciding when to treat a set of items as a multipart work where they all share the same title proper and when to treat them as a series having different titles proper for each part.

(Obviously, it is also possible for items both to be part of a series and to be a multipart work, but this does not usually present any additional problems.)

The only guidance that AACR2 offers on this is in Chapter 13, **13.3A** where one would not really expect to find it. Here we are told: 'If the item is part of a monographic series or a multipart monograph and has a title not dependent on that of the comprehensive item, prepare an analytical entry consisting of a complete bibliographic description of the part. Give details of the comprehensive item in the series area.'

Most people when they talk about analytical entries mean making entries for individual works *within a physical item*, and because of this I think that few would look in Chapter 13 for guidance on multipart works and series.

There is a range of different possibilities. At one end of the spectrum we have items which are clearly part of a series, but where each item is quite independent. In these cases no one would think of treating the series statement as the title proper.

Examples
(Fig. 4.2, p. 28)

        The natural history of moles

(Fig. 4.7, p. 37)

        Riches of the wild

(Fig. 4.14, p. 48)

        Constitutional & administrative law

(Fig. 5.13, p. 116)

        The Freedom of Information Act 2000

In these cases it is inconceivable—I hope!—that anyone would want to make the title proper

        Christopher Helm mammal series

        Images of Asia

        The Cavendish Q & A series

        Butterworths new law guides

turning the existing title proper into a part title.

At the other end of the spectrum is something like a 12-volume encyclopaedia, where although there may be different letters or volume titles printed on the title pages of the volumes, no one would wish to catalogue each volume separately under its individual title and turn the main title into a series statement.

(Neither am I suggesting that you would create separate catalogue records for each volume in any way. Normally you would make one record, and indicate in the Physical description area the number of volumes.)

I hope we all agree on these two extremes. It is some of the things that come in between that are the problem.

It is difficult to give definite guidance about this, but the following pointers may be helpful, as long as you remember that they are only *suggestive*, they are not hard and fast rules:

- Have the individual parts got titles of their own? – or do they just have designations like 'Volume 1' or 'Book 6'? If they do not have titles you *must* treat them as a multipart work, because otherwise you will have no title proper at all.
- Do the parts clearly form a unit which has been divided physically just for convenience, e.g. a Report with an Appendix volume? This almost certainly implies a multipart work.
- Have the individual parts got *distinctive* titles? – or do they just have vague titles like 'Appendix' or '1918-1945'? If they do not have distinctive titles it is likely that you should treat them as a multipart work, because such titles make little sense on their own. But this is not infallible.
- Do the titles of the individual parts appear on the cover or spine? If not, it is likely that this is a multipart work.
- Is there any significance to the order of reading the various parts? – e.g., do they tell a chronological story, or do they form a progressive sequence in terms of content? If there is no significance, it is probable that you will treat them as a series.
- Consider the typographic layout of the chief source of information. A multipart title is much more likely to be given emphasis than a series title, though this is by no means conclusive.
- Do the volumes form a set which *look* as though they belong together and which you would expect to sit together on the shelves? If so, it is likely that they should be treated as a multipart work.
- Does it appear that the number of volumes or units is finite? This could indicate a multipart work, but is not infallible. Series, on the other hand, tend to be more indefinite.
- Are all the parts by the same author? This may be a factor in deciding that they are a multipart work rather than a series.
- Do all the volumes deal with the same subject? Would they all be shelved together? If so, this may be an indication that they form a multipart work.
- Do you actually want to shelve the individual parts separately or together? This is a classification question, but it may be a deciding factor in some cases.
- Has the apparent series title got numbers? If it has *not*, it is most likely that you will treat it as a series, not a multipart title.
- But conversely: has the apparent series got *very high* numbers? This is likely to indicate a series, rather than a multipart title.

THE CITY OF LONDON

Volume IV
A Club No More 1945–2000

————

DAVID KYNASTON

Published by Pimlico 2002

Copyright © David Kynaston 2001

First published in Great Britain by Chatto & Windus 2001
Pimlico edition 2002

Pimlico
Random House, 20 Vauxhall Bridge Road,
London SW1V 2SA

title page
verso

PIMLICO

Fig. 6.1

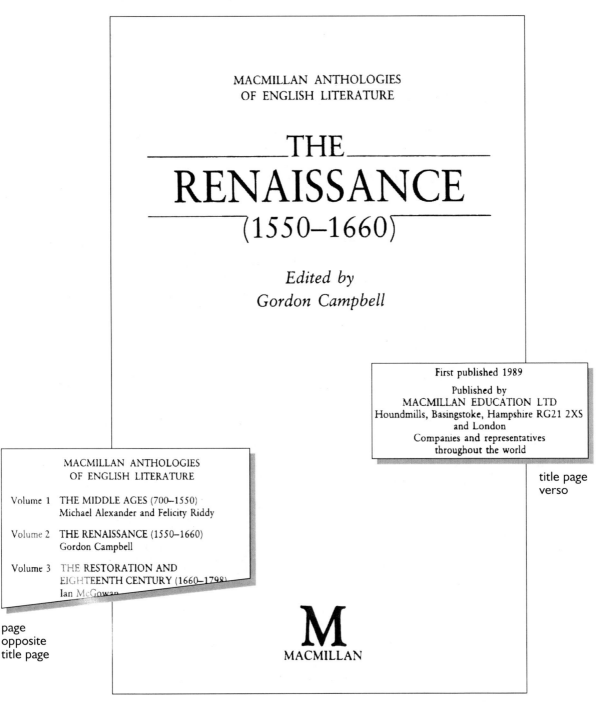

MACMILLAN ANTHOLOGIES
OF ENGLISH LITERATURE

THE
RENAISSANCE
(1550–1660)

Edited by
Gordon Campbell

First published 1989

Published by
MACMILLAN EDUCATION LTD
Houndmills, Basingstoke, Hampshire RG21 2XS
and London
Companies and representatives
throughout the world

title page
verso

MACMILLAN ANTHOLOGIES
OF ENGLISH LITERATURE

Volume 1   THE MIDDLE AGES (700–1550)
Michael Alexander and Felicity Riddy

Volume 2   THE RENAISSANCE (1550–1660)
Gordon Campbell

Volume 3   THE RESTORATION AND
EIGHTEENTH CENTURY (1660–1798)
Ian McGowan

page
opposite
title page

M
MACMILLAN

Fig. 6.2

- Does the name of a publisher appear in the 'series' title? This is often an indicator of a series.
- Does the word 'series' appear in the series title? If so, in most cases you will treat it as a series. Even this is not infallible, however.
- Is the apparent series title of little significance? This is likely to indicate that it should be treated as a series, not a multipart title.

Examples

(Fig. 6.1, p. 132)

```
The City of London. Volume IV, A club no more
 : 1945-2000 / David Kynaston
```

This would perhaps more commonly be done as

```
The City of London. Vol. 4: A club no more :
1945-2000 / David Kynaston
```

This is the final part of a set of four books all dealing with the same subject, by the same person. The general appearance gives priority to the multipart title wherever it appears.

(Fig. 6.2, p. 133)

```
The Renaissance : 1550-1660 / edited by Gordon
Campbell. - Basingstoke : Macmillan Education,
1989. - xxvii, 415 p. ; 22 cm. - (Macmillan
anthologies of English literature ; v. 2)
```

Here typographic prominence is given to the part title. The series title is comparable with many other publishers' series. Nevertheless a case could be made for doing it the other way.

(Fig. 6.3, opposite)

```
Oxford English dictionary additions series. Volume
1 / edited by John Simpson and Edmund Weiner
```

A good example of when not to rely on wording! Although the word 'series' appears in the title this cannot possibly be treated as a series, because then there would be no title.

Some series, such as *The Victoria county history*, have been going for so long that the titles and series statements in different volumes have been presented in many different ways.

No guidance that I could give you would enable you to come at a completely consistent method for cataloguing these volumes. If you are

OXFORD ENGLISH DICTIONARY ADDITIONS SERIES

EDITED BY

JOHN SIMPSON AND EDMUND WEINER

———

VOLUME 1

———

Oxford University Press, Walton Street, Oxford OX2 6DP
*Oxford New York Toronto
Delhi Bombay Calcutta Madras Karachi
Kuala Lumpur Singapore Hong Kong Tokyo
Nairobi Dar es Salaam Cape Town
Melbourne Auckland Madrid*

*and associated companies in
Berlin Ibadan*

Oxford is a trade mark of Oxford University Press

*Published in the United States
by Oxford University Press Inc., New York*

© *Oxford University Press 1993*

title page
verso

CLARENDON PRESS · OXFORD

1993

Fig. 6.3

lucky, you may be able to do each set of county volumes consistently, though even this is doubtful.

Non-book materials
Cartographic materials

There is a rule that allows you to treat a whole set of maps as one item if you wish, and simply create one record for the set. This may be useful in some circumstances, but you will need to consider whether you might be better off with separate records for retrieval or circulation purposes.

3.0J1

Videos

I single out videos from other non-book materials as being of particular concern in libraries, largely because of the amount of off-air recording that takes place.

Here again we find the same range of multipart titles and series as with books. The matter was discussed in some detail by Turp (1992), and the main recommendations would be:

- Treat indefinite series like 'Panorama' as series statements, so that the title proper is the title of the individual programme.
- In the case of indefinite series that lack individual programme titles treat the series name as a multipart title, and construct individual programme titles in square brackets.
- Treat most other series as multipart works. Most of these will have a finite number of programmes, often showing a progression in the subject-matter.
- If necessary, add programme numbers in square brackets to preserve the sequence of the programmes.

Change of title between parts

21.2B2

If the title proper changes between parts, you use the title proper of the *first* part as the title of the whole, unless a later title comes to predominate. In that case you use the later title for the whole.

Change of persons or bodies responsible between parts

21.3A2

Again, if there is a change, you enter the whole set under the heading for the *first* part, unless a later person or body comes to predominate. In that case you change the main entry to the one appropriate for the later parts, and make an added entry for the name that was on the first part.

7 Headings for persons

Having looked at main and added entries in AACR2 Chapter 21 we now, at last, come to the rules for establishing the actual forms of name to be used. Chapter 22 deals with personal names, and Chapters 23 and 24 with the various kinds of corporate body.

These rules, of course, apply whether the access point is main entry or added entry, as we always use the same form of name for the same thing.

MARC: use 100 for main entry, 700 for added entry

Choice of name

As with the other chapters, we still have a little preliminary work to do before we actually arrive at the form of name as it is to appear in a heading. That is to say, we have to choose the version of the name that is to be used as the basis for the heading. You can most easily understand this by means of an example:

William Shakespeare's name has been spelt in various different ways over the years, such as

William Shakespeare
William Shakspere

and different editions of his works have used different forms of the name. But we want all his works to be entered under the *same* form of name, and this means deciding on one of them. The purpose of the first part of this chapter is to help you decide which name to use as the basis for the heading if a person uses, or is known by, more than one.

In looking at a person's name we have to use 'the name by which he or she is commonly known'. This is meant to be a simple rule (and in application it usually is), enabling you to base the heading on the form of name by which the person is known, even if you know something about the person which perhaps other people don't.

For example, you may know that the name is really a pseudonym. But if this is how the author chooses to be known, it is nobody's business whether it is a pseudonym or not. Likewise, because Hilda

22.1A

Doolittle chose to be known as H.D. that is the basis of the form of her name in a catalogue.

If you look at the examples under this rule you will see further cases where people are known by a form of name which is not the 'official' form, e.g.

22.1A, examples

> Jimmy Carter
> Capability Brown

Some of these may seem surprising, because we get used to finding out what people's 'real' names are when they are given a knighthood or other honour. I'm sure you can remember your surprise when you learned that Jimmy Young's real name was Leslie. In cataloguing, what matters is that we use the form of name by which they are normally known.

There is, however, an exception to this, and this concerns certain words like 'Sir', 'Dame', 'Mrs.' and similar, which may appear as part of the name. You have to omit these, however much they appear to be part of the name used by the person, *unless*

22.1C

- the name would otherwise consist of a surname only, e.g.

> Miss Read

or

- the name is that of a married woman who is using her husband's first name or initials, e.g.

> Mrs. Henry Wood

Determining which name to use

How do you decide *which* is the correct name to use, if the person is known by more than one? This can be quite a complicated question, and there are several rules that cover its different aspects.

For most authors you use 'the chief sources of information of works by that person issued in his or her language'. This is all very well for writers but is not very helpful for people like artists, who may not have actually written books. The rule therefore continues by allowing you to use *reference sources* issued in the person's language or country of residence or activity. 'Reference sources' means practically anything that you might use for reference, so it is a very broad term.

22.1B

22.1B fn. 1

The rules about diacritics and hyphens are here just to tell you that you *should* add these things if they do not appear in the source of information you

22.1D

are using. This is comparable to the situation in transcribing elements of the description.

1.0G1

Returning to forms of name, this is only a start. Although perhaps most authors always use the same form of name whenever they write, some may use *different names* or *different forms of the same name*, and these possibilities also have to be covered.

Choice between different names

22.2
22.2A

The first part of this rule is rather peculiar, because no examples are given, and it is difficult to know what kind of name is meant. The rule itself, however, is clear enough. You have an order of priorities, which is:

- the name by which the person is clearly most commonly known
- the name that appears most frequently in the person's works
- the name that appears most frequently in reference sources
- the latest name.

All this of course ties in with *authority control* (see pp. 175–80).

In the above cases the assumption is that the various names are all *real*. The next parts of the rule deal with pseudonyms and cases where writers deliberately use different names for different kinds of work ('separate bibliographic identities').

Pseudonyms

22.2B

Because the basis of this chapter is that we use the name by which the writer wishes to be known, it follows that we continue to do this when a writer chooses to use a pseudonym. If you think about it from a practical point of view, this is a very sensible rule, because it is what is bound to happen by default if you don't know that a particular name is a pseudonym. If you do know the real name, make a cross-reference from it, in case any catalogue users look there.

They might do this, because some older catalogue rules required entry under real name, and some reference books occasionally do this.

Separate bibliographic identities

22.2B2

The rule about pseudonyms refers to writers who use *only* their pseudonym. This rule covers those who use more than one name because they write different kinds of book and have established separate 'bibliographic identities' for the different kinds of work. As you might expect, you enter each item under the name that the writer used in that item, and make cross-references between them so that users can link up all the works if they want to.

The only reason that there is a separate section on 'Contemporary authors' is to allow for the fact that such writers may not have had time to *establish* separate bibliographic identities. In effect the rule amounts to the same thing as the previous one.

22.2B3

Change of name

22.2C

Note the difference between this and the preceding rules. Those rules dealt with authors who use more than one name *at the same time*, whereas this deals with different names at *different times*. Note the consequent different result: now you have to establish *one* form of name and use it. This will be the latest form, 'unless there is reason to believe that an earlier name will persist as the name by which the person is better known'.

22.2C1

How you are meant to decide whether there is 'reason to believe' is not clear, because whether a name persists will only become apparent with hindsight. Luckily this is a problem which arises very seldom.

Choice between different forms of the same name

22.3

This is a much more common problem than having to choose between actual different names. Most authors probably do try to use the same form of name in all their works, but occasionally differences occur, sometimes accidentally, and sometimes due to the policy of the publishers. It is therefore not uncommon to have what is obviously the same name appearing in varying degrees of fullness.

Again there is an order of priority:

22.3A1

- the commonest form
- if no one form predominates, use the latest
- if in doubt about which is the latest, use the fullest.

The problem with this is that if the rule is followed correctly it should mean that headings are constantly being changed in any authority file or catalogue.

For instance, looking at the second example:

- if Morris West writes one book, the heading for his name will be based on the form 'Morris West';
- if he then writes another calling himself Morris L. West, we now have one of each, which means that no one form predominates; we there-

fore have to choose the latest, which means that we must change to heading to be based on 'Morris L. West'

- if he then writes a third book and calls himself Morris West again we shall have to change the heading back so that it is based on that, because this is now the one most commonly found.

This is what ought to happen, but in reality it is doubtful whether it often does, because it involves considerable work. What usually happens is that once a heading has got into the authority file it tends to stay in that form.

Different languages

22.3B

There are several special rules to cater for people who have had names in more than one language. You will probably not need these very often.

Classical Latin names

Notice that here, if there is a well established English form of a Latin writer's name, you use it; otherwise use the full Latin form.

22.3B3

This is a silly rule and very inconsistent. It is just an accident of linguistics that 'Horace' looks quite different from 'Horatius', whereas 'Cicero' looks identical to 'Cicero'. The result is that, while we can use 'Horace' on its own as the basis for that heading, we have to use 'Marcus Tullius Cicero' for Cicero.

Entry element

22.4

So far this chapter has looked only at the *choice* of name to be used as the basis for the heading. We now at last come to *how* it is entered.

The general rule, as you might expect, is that a person's name is entered under the element under which the name would normally appear in 'authoritative alphabetic lists' in his or her language or country of residence or activity. The final part of the sentence may seem rather vague, but it is deliberately designed to be flexible, according to requirements of the particular name.

If the person's preference is known to be different, it should be followed. This may be difficult to find out, and it is one of the cases where you may find it helpful to read the dust-jacket and any other accompanying information.

Some examples show how the rule works in practice. They start with a name where the entry element is actually the *first* element, in which case we simply enter the name in direct order as it stands.

22.4B1

If the entry element is a surname, you put a comma after it before adding the rest of it. Again this is quite unusual in most western-

22.4B2

language catalogues.

    If the entry element is not the first element when the name is writ-ten in direct order, you transpose the elements so as to bring the surname to the beginning. Follow it with a comma, space, and the inverted part of the name. In practice, in normal work in European lan-guages, this is the kind of name you will most commonly meet.

22.4B3

Cross-references

Note that from this point on, in the rules, you will see many examples of instructions about making cross-references. These are all marked with an *x*, which means 'make a cross-reference from' the name following.

MARC:
100 or 700, first
indicator 1

$a for surname.
No subfield code
for inverted
element: simply
add comma and
space.

Entry under surname

22.5

This of course is the type of name that we are most familiar with in western countries. Single-word surnames are easy to deal with. We use the surname as the entry element, and invert the other part(s) to go after it.

22.4B3

Examples

    (Fig. 4.1, p. 26)

        Henig, Martin

    (Fig. 4.2, p. 28)

        Gorman, Martyn L.
        Stone, R. David

    (Fig. 4.3, p. 29)

        Clifton, Robert T.

    (Fig. 4.11, p. 43)

        Husain, B. M. C.

Note that in this last example we need to put spaces *between* all the ini-tials. This is quite contrary to AACR2, but is required in order to make names file correctly in an alphabetical sequence.

    Notice the difference from the statement of responsibility, where you do *not* put spaces (p. 44).

MARC:
100 or 700, first
indicator 1

Surnames consisting of more than one word

But what about surnames consisting of more than one word, like Dun-can Smith or de la Mare? What do we do with these?

The answer is given in two rules:

- Compound surnames   **22.5C**
- Names with separately written prefixes.   **22.5D**

In both cases we find that the fundamental principle is that we do *whatever the author would do* in his or her own language.

MARC:
100 or 700, first
indicator 1

Compound surnames   **22.5C**

This rule covers the kinds of name where two or more *whole words* are involved. As usual, preference is given to the form *which the person prefers*. **22.5C2** Obviously you will not often know this, and so the rest of the rule tells you what to do when you do not. Look in reference sources and find out how the name is listed.

If the name is hyphenated, treat the whole compound as the surname. **22.5C3**

Examples

(Fig. 5.13, p. 116)

```
Pitt-Payne, Timothy
```

(Fig. 5.14, p. 118)
```
Graham-Dixon, Andrew
```

There are then some rather involved rules about compound names, with a distinction being made according to whether the name of a married woman is involved. **22.5C4**

Sometimes you may suspect that a surname is a compound name but have no evidence of this. In this case you must treat it as if it is *not* a compound name. This is because some people like to include their middle name but would not regard it as in any way part of their surname. **22.5C6**

So, because we know that Iain Duncan Smith is always referred to as 'Mr Duncan Smith', and is so listed in *Who's who*, we can tell that the surname is Duncan Smith and enter this name accordingly. But if he were simply referred to as 'Mr Smith' we would have to assume that Smith was his surname.

Sometimes a person starts using his or her middle name and it gradually turns into a compound surname. Edward Burne Jones was originally known as Edward Jones.

Examples
```
Layzell Ward, Patricia
Neville Rolfe, Eustace
```

MARC:
100 or 700, first
indicator 1

Surnames with separately written prefixes   22.5D

This set of rules deals with those names that consist not of two or more *whole words* but of one or more prefixes followed by a whole word, such as de la Mare, la Fontaine. It is a difficult set of rules, because the rules vary according to the language of the person concerned, which means that it is impossible to give catalogue users a general rule as to how to look such names up.

You cannot expect to learn all the rules, but you must be aware that they are there. Gradually you should become familiar with the rules for English and the commoner European languages, such as French and German.

English

English is very simple: you enter under the prefix. This means that de la Mare goes under D, not L or M. This is quite easy to understand and remember.

Example
(Fig. 5.8, p. 99)

```
De Grey, Roger
```

Note that *all* headings have to start with a capital letter, regardless of   A.2A1
the usage of the person or body concerned.

There are more problems with French and German, where the entry point will depend on the nature of the prefix.

French

If the prefix is an article, *or a contraction of an article and a preposition,* enter under the prefix. Otherwise you use the part of the name that follows the preposition. This seems confusing, but it is in accordance with normal French national practice.

It means that if Walter de la Mare had been French, he would have been entered under La Mare, whereas Daphne du Maurier would have remained the same, under Du Maurier, whether she were French or English.

German

This is rather like French, except that an article is never used as the entry point.

Italian

This is even more complicated because it depends on when the person lived. For medieval names the rules give up and tell you to look at reference sources. The result of this, usually, is that Leonardo da Vinci goes under Leonardo, whereas if he had been alive now he would have been entered under Da Vinci, Leonardo.

Nationality unclear

A problem sometimes arises in that you cannot be certain of the nationality of the person concerned. This is a particular problem with German- or Dutch-looking names starting with 'von' and 'van' which are quite likely to belong to English speakers who are resident in Britain or the USA. If there is every reason to believe that the person belongs to an English-speaking country, you should treat the name as being English. If, on the other hand, the work appears to have been translated from German or Dutch, or gives other indications that the writer is not English-speaking, you should treat the name as German or Dutch.

Other kinds of prefixes   **22.5D2**

Some languages use prefixes that are not prepositions or articles, and these are all treated as part of the name and used as the entry point.

Titles of nobility   **22.6,**

There are several rules which relate to titles of nobility, and it will be   **22.12**
more convenient to look at them all together.

The first thing to remember is that you only use a title of nobility as the basis for a heading if the person concerned actually uses it in his or her works (or, in the case of someone who is not an author, is commonly known by it). For example, P. D. James, although she is Baroness James of Holland Park, does not use the title in her works, and you can therefore ignore it.

You need to be clear about which part of the name is which. Everyone with a title has an ordinary surname, and the title of nobility is additional to this. To confuse things further, sometimes the title of nobility is identical to the surname. This is increasingly common now that most people enter the House of Lords by being appointed rather than inheriting a title.

In the example

       Byron, George Gordon Byron, <u>Baron</u>   **22.6A1** there are three elements, in this order:

1. the title of nobility
2. all the first names and surname in direct order (in this case the surname is identical to the title of nobility)
3. the term of rank.

Sometimes the title of nobility includes the name of a place, as in the case of Baroness James of Holland Park. In these cases the 'territorial designation', as it is called, is added *directly to the title of nobility*, rather than being put at the end as you might expect.   **22.6B1**

You need to be aware of this when you are browsing on names in an online catalogue, because if the surname is fairly common the heading you are looking for may not be where you expect it.

Titles of nobility may involve rather more research than ordinary names, because we are required to add the whole of the personal name apart from any unused forenames. The sources of information in the item will probably not give the necessary details.   **22.6A1**

This is a strange rule, which is contrary to the general principle of using the form of name preferred by the person concerned.

Examples
(Fig. 4.7, p. 37)

```
/ Earl of Cranbrook
```

In this example we have a statement of responsibility where the author has clearly decided to use his title of nobility. We shall therefore make the entry point

```
Cranbrook
```

but we need further details to add to it and complete the heading; we need to find out his first name and family name in order to complete the heading. This results in:

MARC: use $c
for *Earl of*

```
Cranbrook, Gathorne Gathorne-Hardy, Earl of
```

Whether we go further than this depends on whether we have anyone else in our authority file with the same name.

(Fig. 10.4, p. 195)

```
/ compiled and with an introduction by the
Earl of Birkenhead
```

This time the name proves to be:

```
Birkenhead, Frederick Winston Furneaux Smith,
Earl of, 1907-1975
```

MARC:
100 or 700, first
indicator 0

Entry under given name, etc.

22.8

'Given name' is a way of saying 'first name', i.e. the name that you are given, rather than the one you are born with. It avoids using terms like christian name, which is exclusive, or forename, which implies that a surname is following.

You are not likely to need this rule very often in an ordinary library of modern material. The kinds of people who are usually known by their given name are

- kings and queens
- saints (but not all of them)
- popes.

We start with some saints, including

$c for addition

```
John, the Baptist
```

though it is hard to see what he is doing here in a set of rules that deals only with authors, not subjects.

You are unlikely to come across Paulus Diaconus, but if you do, remember to make all the cross-references.

$b for roman
numeral

Many such names require a roman numeral following immediately upon the name.

C.2A1

MARC:
100 or 700, first
indicator 0

Entry under initials, letters or numerals

22.10

It is unusual nowadays for anyone to use only initials, or letters or numerals, but you may come across such writers if you are dealing with older works.

The main rule is that you use the initials in *direct order*, not inverted, but that you make a cross-reference from the inverted form.

22.10A

The cross-references prescribed here are rather odd. The general purpose of a cross-reference is that you make it *once*, regardless of how many times the name might occur in your catalogue. But in this particular case you are instructed to make a *name-title* cross-reference for *each work*.

The reason for this is not given, but it is perhaps to cater for the fact that the same set of initials might be used by more than one person and it would otherwise be difficult to differentiate them.

MARC:
100 or 700, first
indicator 0

Entry under phrase

22.11

This kind of name is even rarer, and you will seldom see any when dealing with ordinary modern books. It is a rather confusing sequence of rules, which it would be impossible to memorize. You need to look carefully at the actual wording if ever you need to use this rule. This accounts for the apparently odd difference between

      `Father Time`   **22.11A**

and

      `Jemima, `<u>`Aunt`</u>   **22.11B**

use $c for the addition

Don't forget that this rule also includes words or phrases that are used in place of an ordinary name, such as 'a Physician'. In this case the heading is   **22.11D**

      `Physician`

Remember, however, that this form of entry is only used if we don't know the real name of the author.   **21.5C**

Additions to names
22.12–22.16

AACR2 contains quite a long group of rules under this heading. I have tried to include most of them under other headings because I think it is more useful to consider them in relation to the kinds of name to which they relate.

The question of what constitutes an addition to a name is not clear and does not seem well thought out. Surely many of these so called additions are simply parts of the existing name that have to be inverted. The fact that they are not forenames makes a difference to the layout but does not necessarily mean that they are additions.

MARC: 100 or 700, first indicator 1

Married women
22.15B

If a married woman is identified by her husband's first names or initials, you have to add the necessary 'Mrs.' at the end of the heading, e.g.

Use $c for *Mrs.*

      `Wood, Henry, `<u>`Mrs`</u>`.`

You are unlikely to find this kind of name in modern works because few women now wish to be known by their husbands' initials.

Saints
Essentially there are two kinds of name for saints:

MARC: 100 or 700, first indicator 0

1. Those consisting of christian name only
Enter under christian name, with or without the kinds of addition which have already been mentioned, and including the word 'Saint'.   **22.8A1** **22.13B**

$c for the
addition

Examples

```
Alban, Saint
Francis, of Assisi, Saint
```

MARC:
100 or 700, first
indicator 1

2. *Those with a conventional surname also*

Enter as an ordinary inverted name, but add 'Saint' at the end of the heading.   **22.13A**

$c for the
addition

Example

```
More, Thomas, Saint
```

Notice that if you have to differentiate between identical names of saints, you use 'any other suitable word or phrase necessary'. This contrasts with the more general rules (see below) for distinguishing identical names.

MARC: use
whatever would
be appropriate
for the name,
and add $c for
(*Spirit*).

Spirits

We have already seen that items purporting to come from spirits are entered under the heading for the spirit. Here we see what the form of that name is: it is the same as the heading for the person, but has '(*Spirit*)'   **22.14** added to it for differentiation. This means that in a catalogue such items will appear after the items by the living person, but not interfiled with them.

Distinguishing identical names   **22.17–**

This is a very important aspect of cataloguing, and relates especially   **22.18** to authority control (see pp. 178–80).

Many names are unique, but probably most are not. Luckily not everyone with a common name like John Smith does anything to justify ending up in a catalogue, but there are still plenty that do, and, if we are going to achieve the aim of collocating works by an individual author, we need to try to separate the different persons involved.

We have already seen how to do this with saints. For more normal names, there are two principal methods, namely

• adding dates to the heading
• adding a fuller form of name to the heading.

The problem with the rules is that they do not state clearly which takes precedence.

MARC:
$d

Dates

22.17A

The aim here is add a date of birth and/or death to the heading. There are various possibilities:

- year of birth followed by dash (if the person is still alive)
- years of birth and death, separated by a dash
- year of birth only, preceded by '*b.*' (if the person is clearly dead but the date of death is unknown)
- year, month and day (if there is more than one person with the same year); notice that year and month alone are not used.

In any of these cases it may be necessary to include such qualifications as '*ca.*' before a date or '?' after it, to indicate uncertainty.

See the full rule for further detail of unusual cases.

For more suggestions about possible sources of this type of information see p. 180.

Notice that there is an *option* of adding the dates anyway, even if they are not at present needed for differentiation purposes. The British Library and the Library of Congress have both been following this option to some extent for some years now, when they have been aware of the dates.

MARC:
$q(   )

Fuller forms

22.18

A fuller form of name is *normally* used only when one or more of the person's given names are represented by initials, e.g. D. H. Lawrence, or T. S. Eliot. In such cases you can *add* the full names (in parentheses) after the rest of the heading, e.g.

```
Eliot, T. S. (Thomas Stearns)
```

Notice that you must *not* simply convert the initials *into* the fuller forms; you have to give the initials first, because they are the form of name which the person has chosen to use.

The first few examples are clear enough, because they represent spelt-out forms of initials. What introduces uncertainty is the second sentence in the second paragraph of this rule, and the related examples, where a further name *which is not represented by initials at all* is added.

We are surely then entitled to ask: why in these cases are we adding an extra name *rather than* using dates of birth and death, as in the John Smith examples?

To this I think the answer is simply that it depends on what

22.18A

information you can find. In my view it is preferable to add dates rather than names which are not represented by initials, but there may be occasions where this is all you can do.

Notice, again, that there is an *option* of adding the spelt-out names even if it is not necessary for identification purposes, but that in this case you must not add unused forenames.

Dates and fuller forms

In practice, because the national libraries are tending to follow the options, you will often see headings which include *both* dates *and* spelt-out forenames. In the case of common names, they are often both likely to be needed anyway.

Examples

```
Smith, J. H. (James Harold), 1927-
Smith, J. H. (James Hiram), 1916-
Smith, J. H. (John Henry), 1902-
Smith, J. H. (John Henry), 1928-
Smith, J. H. (John Hilary), 1928-
```

But

```
Rowling, J. K.
```

appears thus in the Library of Congress authorities list, even though her full names and date of birth are also recorded.

Other distinguishing terms

Occasionally you can use other kinds of addition to distinguish identical names.

The first of these applies to persons entered under the given, or only, name, e.g. **22.19A**

MARC:
$c(   )

```
Thomas (Anglo-Norman poet)
```

You will not see many of these in dealing with modern publications.

The second is more likely to occur, but is still rare. You may add some kind **22.19B** of qualifier provided that 'it appears with the name in works by the person or in reference sources'. In other words, if someone calls himself 'Captain John Smith' and you can't find any better way to distinguish him, you *are* allowed to put '*Captain*' after the name. What you are *not* allowed to do is make up qualifiers of this sort; they *must* appear somewhere in conjunction with the name. In practice you seldom get the opportunity to use this rule, which is a pity.

Undifferentiated names   **22.20**

After all this effort to distinguish identical names it seems a pity that we have to end up with a rule that allows us to put them all together after all. But this is inevitable, as there will be many occasions where you simply cannot find out a date or anything else suitable, and the time spent on it would not justify the result.

We will therefore sometimes end up with more than one person entered under the same heading. Although AACR2 does not say so, because it says nothing about filing, the implication of this is that all the titles will be interfiled in a single sequence, even if the subject matter might lead you to think you can group them together in some other way.

8 Headings for corporate bodies

MARC: Use 110 for main entry, 710 for added entries (except for conferences: see below).

We have seen the definition of a corporate body, and you have to keep this in mind. In this section we look at the forms of name to be used for corporate bodies. **21.1B1**

I shall not entirely follow the order of AACR2 here, because it is more helpful to bring certain topics together which in AACR2 are scattered.

The first part of the chapter covers points which apply to *all* kinds of corporate name; this is then followed by sections on Conferences and Government names specifically.

As you might expect, from what you have seen of personal names, the basic rule in establishing the form of name for a corporate body is that you use the name by which it is commonly identified. In order to determine what this is, you use, in this order of preference: **24.1A**

- items issued by the body
- reference sources.

Punctuation and spacing   **24.1A**

Notice the rule about full stops and spaces in headings. If you have a group of initials with full stops, do *not* put a space after each full stop until you come to the *last one*, the one immediately preceding the rest of the name. You would therefore put, e.g.

> ✔ F.W. Woolworth Company

not

> ✘ F. W. Woolworth Company

Notice that the ampersand should be used only if it is used in the name of the body concerned; it should not be introduced as an abbreviation.

In some systems there is a policy of converting it into 'and' because sometimes it causes difficulties in filing.

All kinds of elements may appear in the name of a corporate body.

MARC: There is no special coding for such elements.

This includes elements in parentheses, if they happen to be part of the official name.

Examples

```
Marlborough Fine Art (London) Ltd
Southwick (Sussex) Society
```

MARC: Such additions also have no special coding.

Distinguish this kind of element in parentheses from the *additions* that you sometimes have to make to names to differentiate different bodies with the same name (see below, pp. 157–9).

Capitalization

Remember that when you are constructing a heading for a corporate body, *of whatever kind*, you follow the rules appropriate for the language in question. This means that in English you would put capital letters for the *principal* words in the name (not for words like 'and', 'of', 'the', etc.). In many languages you would not use capitals. In French there are special rules. In all cases you must consult Appendix A for instructions on each language, and remember that the rules apply to corporate names whether they appear as headings or *elsewhere in the record*.

A18.E1

A39.B1
App. A

Order of elements in name

MARC: Beware of old information which implies that such inversions can occur. This is based on old pre-AACR2 rules.

One thing which sometimes confuses beginners is the fact that initials and forenames that appear at the beginning of a corporate name are *not* inverted but are kept in direct order. This of course is the opposite to what happens with headings for most *personal* names. It means that if a *firm* is called 'John Smith' it will have as the basis of its heading

```
John Smith
```

(we would have to add some explanation to it: see p. 158), whereas a *person* called John Smith would be

```
Smith, John
```

This can be unsatisfactory in the case of a one-person business, where it may be difficult to distinguish between the person and the business.

There is only one exception to this, and it applies only to certain types of name in certain languages. It never arises with English names.

24.5C2

Changes of name

24.1C1

As with persons, corporate bodies can change their names. Unlike persons, however, in this case we do *not* establish a single form of name for the body: we use the different forms which apply to each publication.

In order to help users find all the items of such corporate bodies you must make cross-references between them. You may either do simple 'see also' references or make a longer, explanatory reference which gives a brief history of the changes of name. If you choose the latter option, just keep to straightforward statements of fact.

See Chapter 9 of this book for more information on cross-references in relation to authority control.

Variant names   24.2

This rule differs from the previous one, in that it deals with corporate bodies where different names appear *at the same time* rather than changing over time.

Use, in this order of precedence:

- the form appearing in the chief source of information of items
- the name presented formally
- the predominant form
- a form that differentiates the body from others with the same or similar names.

For most organizations there is no problem, but with the increasing use of acronyms it can sometimes be difficult to know which is really the formal or official name.

Sometimes an organization may have a very long formal name which in practice is never used.

Names in different languages   24.3A,
                                                                     24.3B
Most English organizations naturally have English names, but if you start to deal with international organizations, or even with organizations in bilingual countries, like Wales or Canada, you need to be aware of how to decide which language to use.

In choosing which language to use, follow this order of precedence:

- use the official language of the body
- if there is more than one official language, and one of them is English, use English
- if none of them is English and you do not know which is the official language, use the form which is predominantly used in the organization's publications

Springer
Berlin
Heidelberg
New York
Barcelona
Budapest
Hong Kong
London
Milan
Paris
Singapore
Tokyo

page
opposite
title page

Advances in
Artificial Intelligence

12th Biennial Conference of the Canadian Society
for Computational Studies of Intelligence, AI'98
Vancouver, BC, Canada, June 18-20, 1998
Proceedings

Lecture Notes in Artificial Intelligence

Subseries of Lecture Notes in Computer Science
Edited by J. G. Carbonell and J. Siekmann

Lecture Notes in Computer Science
Edited by G. Goos, J. Hartmanis and J. van Leeuwen

half title
page

Series Editors
Jaime G. Carbonell, Carnegie Mellon University, Pittsburgh, PA, USA
Jörg Siekmann, University of Saarland, Saarbrücken, Germany

Volume Editors

Robert E. Mercer
Department of Computer Science, University of Western Ontario
London, ON, N6A 5B7, Canada

Eric Neufeld
Department of Computer Science, University of Saskatchewan
57 Campus Drive, Saskatoon, SK, S7N 5A9, Canada

© Springer-Verlag Berlin Heidelberg 1998

title page
verso

 Springer

Fig. 8.1

- if in doubt, use English, French, German, Spanish or Russian in that order
- failing even that, use whichever language's English name comes first in alphabetical order.

Note that there is an alternative rule which allows you to use a translated form of a foreign-language name if you think it will be more useful to the users of your catalogue. This is particularly useful in cases which involve transliteration, such as Russian or Japanese. **24.3A1 fn. 7**

Example
(Fig. 8.1, opposite)

✔ Canadian Society for Computational Studies of Intelligence

✘ Société canadienne pour l'étude de l'intelligence par ordinateur

Here there are two official languages, and so English is used as the heading. Make a cross-reference from the French form. (Notice incidentally the differing systems of capitalization.) **A.18E1, A.39B1, A.39A2**

Miscellaneous other types of variant name

The section on variant names continues with a collection of miscellaneous rules that apply in particular circumstances. It is very easy to be misled here and think that these rules cover *all* occurrences of the type of body they mention. They do not; they only apply when any of these types of body have variant names. **24.3B– 24.3G**

Conventional names

It is not easy to know exactly what kinds of name would be covered by this rule, but it does not arise very often. **24.3C1**

Ancient or international bodies

The heading in AACR2 is misleading because the bodies do not have to be both ancient and international; just one of these will do. In fact some of the examples given are neither. **24.3C2**

Religious orders and societies

Again preference is given to English when at all possible. **24.3D1**

Additions to names of bodies

Sometimes the name as it stands is not sufficient to be used as a head- **24.4** ing. The commonest reasons for this are that:

- the name does not look like a corporate body
- there is more than one body with the same name.

We therefore need to add something to the heading,

- to make it clear that the name is in fact that of a corporate body; or
- to differentiate between otherwise identical names.

MARC:
no special
coding: include
as part of $a

Adding something to make clear that the name is that of a corporate body

24.4B1

Add an appropriate term in parentheses, to describe the *kind* of corporate body that it is. The commonest of these is probably '(*Firm*)' which is used especially when a firm's name consists merely of the name of a person.

Notice that whatever word you use it starts with a capital letter.

A.2D1

Example

(Fig. 5.10, p. 103: added entry)

```
Winward Fearon (Firm)
```

Other examples:

```
Anthony's Research (Firm)
Communication Briefings (Firm)
Dire Straits (Musical group)
U2 (Musical group)
U505 (Submarine)
Zacks Investment Research (Firm)
```

Two or more bodies with the same name

It is of course quite common for bodies with the same name to appear in different places or at different times, and this is particularly a problem with non-specific names.

In these cases the first thing you should try to add is a *place name* of some kind.

MARC:
no special
coding: include
as part of $a

If the nature of the organization is national, you naturally add the name of the country; again this is in parentheses, as all additions to a corporate name have to be.

24.4C2

If the body is not national, it is more appropriate to add the name of a local place, usually a town.

24.4C3

The main problem here is knowing exactly what to put. You will see that all the examples shown include the name of the country, or, for the

USA, the state, in addition to the town, village or city. In the case of British places, you include the county *only* if it is necessary to distinguish towns with the same name, such as the various Newports which exist in the British Isles.

The example with '(*Sudbury, England*)' looks odd, because there is certainly more than one Sudbury in England. But you have to remember to look at these additions *in relation to the main part of the name itself.* You therefore have to look at the heading

```
St. Peter's Church
```

and consider whether *that specific name* occurs more than once with the addition '(*Sudbury*)'. In this case the answer presumably is no.

The main thing to bear in mind, as in all cases where you have to establish a authorized name for a body you have not dealt with before, is that you should do something sensible. Add what appears to be necessary in the context of your own authority file. You cannot be expected to consider conflicts of name that may occur in the future.

Sometimes it is more appropriate to add the name of an institution, rather than a place name. This is rare. **24.4C5**

Occasionally place names are unsuitable for distinguishing identical names, because both the organizations are in the same place. In these cases you can use years, and you add them in parentheses in the same way. **24.4C6**

MARC:
no special
coding: include
as part of $a

Notice that this is slightly different from dates added to a *personal* name heading. In that case there are no parentheses.

Omissions from names   24.5

These are relatively uncommon, except perhaps in respect of the first kind:

1. Omit any article that appears at the beginning of a name.   **24.5A1**
   I hope that you would do this naturally. You should not expect to find any names filed under 'The' in a catalogue, and you therefore omit it.

   The problem is with German names, where the omission of the article would normally cause the ending on any adjective to change. You just have to accept this.
2. Omit citations of honours. This seems to apply only to Russian names.   **24.5B1**

3. Omit terms indicating incorporation. This is more common. You omit words like 'Limited' at the end of a name, *unless* the omission   **24.5C1**

would result in something that does not look like the name of a corporate body, in which case you retain it. This of course is to avoid the necessity of adding something like '(*Firm*)' as you would otherwise have to do.

Examples

```
Current Biology Limited
Fischer Fine Art Limited
Imagination Limited
```

If we omitted 'Limited' from any of these, it would not be quite clear that they were names of corporate bodies, and we should therefore have to add '(*Firm*)'.

In some languages the word indicating incorporation comes at the beginning of the name, and in this case you transpose it to the end. This is the only case where any part of a corporate name can be transposed.   **24.5C2**

Names of ships

If a ship has an abbreviation in front of the main words of its name, you omit the abbreviation. In such cases you then have to add '(*Ship*)'   **24.5C4**
at the end of the heading. The same applies to other vessels.

Conferences   **24.7**

Remember that a conference, if it has a name, is a corporate body, which   **21.1B1**
is why there is this special section to deal with the forms of name of conferences.

Always use the most specific name for a conference, if it also has a   **24.3F2**
name as part of a series of conferences.

If it does not have a name, you ignore these rules and treat it as if   **21.1C1**
no conference were involved.

If it has a name, you must be clear as to exactly what the name is. Essentially there are three kinds:

- where there are variant forms of the name and one of them includes the abbreviation for another corporate body, to which the conference is *not* subordinate
- where the conference is *subordinate* to another corporate body, e.g. an annual conference of a particular organization
- where the conference has its own name, and the name has no connexion with any other body.

By far the commonest is the third, but we will look at each.

MARC:
111.2_

1. Where a variant form includes initials

24.3F1

This rule might appear rather abstruse, but in fact it is used quite often. If, after following the rules relating to variant names, you find that you are using as the name of a conference one that includes the initials of an organization, then you include those initials in the name, *unless* the conference is subordinate to the name of the organization.

MARC:
110.2_: use $b
for subordinate
part

2. Where the conference is subordinate to another corporate body

24.13A
Type 6

The commonest instance of this is the Annual Conference of an organization, e.g. (Fig. 8.1, p. 156) '12th Biennial Conference of the Canadian Society for Computational Studies of Intelligence'.

MARC:
111.2_

3. Where the conference has its own name independent of another organization

This is the commonest type of name, and we have already seen some examples, e.g. (Fig. 5.1, p. 89) 'Third International Pineapple Symposium'.

Constructing the heading

Whichever kind of name it is, you have to make certain changes before it is suitable to be used as a heading.

In many cases you will be able to use the name as it stands. Don't forget to capitalize the appropriate words, because this is a corporate body exactly like any other.

In other cases you will have to transpose certain words, and in all cases you will have to *add* elements at the end.

Omissions

24.7A1

Some things have to be removed. They are:

- the number of the conference (e.g. 'Second')
- any word indicating its frequency (e.g. 'Annual')
- the year of the conference.

You strip away any of these words or figures, which leaves you with a shorter form of the conference name.

This applies also when the name of the conference is subordinate to another corporate body.

Examples:

(Fig. 5.1, p. 89)

Name of conference: The Third International Pincapplc Symposium
Name after removal of definite article and number:

```
International Pineapple Symposium
```

(Fig. 8.1, p. 156)

Name of conference: 12th Biennial Conference of the Canadian Society for Computational Studies of Intelligence
Name after removal of number and word denoting frequency:

```
Conference of the Canadian Society for
Computational Studies of Intelligence
```

MARC:
110.2_ using $b
for subordinate
part

In the latter case we then need to make the word 'Conference' subordinate to the name of the Society resulting in:

```
Canadian Society for Computational Studies of
    Intelligence. Conference
```

24.13A
Type 6

Additions

24.7B

Having removed these pieces of information, you have to replace some of them (in a different form) at the end of the heading. You do this by adding the following elements, if appropriate, in this order:

- number
- date
- location.

Many conferences of course have no number, and so you may not need to use this element. In most cases you will add place and date, though occasionally one or other of these elements may not be ascertainable.

However many of the three elements you are able to add, you put them together in a single set of parentheses, separating them with 'space colon space'. Let us look at the three elements in a bit more detail.

MARC:
$n

Number

24.7B2

The thing to note here is that you use the *ordinal* form of the number, and that it *must be in English*, whatever the language of the name of the conference. This is quite bizarre, and I cannot account for it. You will therefore add things like '(2nd : ...)' even if the name of the conference is in a foreign language. And remember that you do not use superscript letters in English ordinal numerals.

C.8A

Examples:
(Fig. 5.1, p. 89)

    International Pineapple Symposium (3rd

(Fig. 8.1, p. 156)

    Canadian Society for Computational Studies of
    Intelligence. Conference (12th

MARC:
$d

Date   24.7B3

All conferences take place at some time, and you should therefore usually be able to add the date. You do this by putting the *year only*, unless you have to distinguish between more than one conference in the same year, in which case you add the month(s) and day(s). If there is really no indication of the date, then of course you cannot add it.

Examples:
(Fig. 5.1, p. 89)

    International Pineapple Symposium (3rd : 1998

(Fig. 8.1, p. 156)

    Canadian Society for Computational Studies of
    Intelligence. Conference (12th : 1998

MARC:
$c

Location   24.7B4

There is some ambiguity in the instructions here, in that it says 'the local place or other location (institution, etc.)'. Personally I should always prefer to put a place rather than an institution, and I think this is justified by the order in which the two possibilities are mentioned, but it seems to be very common to put an institutional name.

I should prefer, for example, to put 'Birmingham' rather than 'University of Birmingham'.

Examples:
(Fig. 5.1, p. 89)

    International Pineapple Symposium (3rd : 1998
    : Pattaya, Thailand)

(Fig. 8.1, p. 156)

    Canadian Society for Computational Studies of
    Intelligence. Conference (12th : 1998 :
    Vancouver, Canada)

There are a couple of extra rules which you ought to be aware of:

24.7B4

- if the heading is for a series of conferences held in different places, do not add the location
- if the location is already included in the name of the conference, do not add it
- if the sessions of a conference were held in two places, put both, and if in three or more, give the first, followed by 'etc.'.

In all cases the form of the place name should follow the instructions in AACR2 Chapter 23.

23

Sometimes beginners get confused about the form of a conference heading. The important thing to remember is that the heading is arranged in a *structured* form, with specific elements which have to be put in a special order. You may need to get information for these elements from any part of the item, and indeed occasionally from external sources.

All this is in contrast with the title page transcription, which must, as always, be based on what is actually on the title page. This means that you will often have a specific date on the title page which has to be converted to the *year only* for the heading.

There is another possible element that sometimes needs to be added to a conference heading, and this is not mentioned here because it falls under the more general rule about making clear that a heading is that of a corporate body. By this I mean that sometimes you may need to add the word '(*Conference*)' if it is not clear from the wording of the heading.

24.4B1

Exhibitions, fairs, festivals, etc.

24.8

MARC:
111.2_

As we have seen (pp. 99–100), it is rare for exhibitions, fairs and festivals to count as corporate bodies, because they are not usually presented as having names. But occasionally you will have to construct a heading for a named exhibition, usually a large international one, such as the Great Exhibition of 1851.

Omissions

24.8A1

This is similar to the rule for conferences, but not the same, because this time you do *not* omit words denoting frequency, or year.

Additions

As with conferences, you may occasionally need to add an explanation such as '(*Exhibition*)' to make it clear what the heading is.

Otherwise you add the elements

24.8B1

- number
- year
- location

in the same way as for conferences.

Miscellaneous other rules about additions and omissions in headings

24.9–
24.11

The rules which follow here cover certain other special situations where you need to add something to a heading. You will seldom need them and it is rather surprising that they are given separately here considering that they do not really add anything to the general rules given earlier.

24.4

Subordinate bodies

24.12

Here we have quite a long sequence of rules which at first seem rather complicated. It is not really as bad as it looks, and to a great extent you can follow common sense.

The first thing to be clear about is that (except for government departments, which are dealt with later) in general, even if a body is subordinate to another, you use *its own name*. This means that you do not usually need to know whether a body is subordinate to another or not. This is a very good thing, as it is increasingly difficult to know whether one body is controlling another, and for cataloguing purposes there is no need to know.

24.12A

You therefore need not consider the fact that the Bodleian Library is part of the University of Oxford. It has its own name, and this is what you will use for the heading.

This is in contrast with many older rules, which required subordinate headings in many cases where they would not now be required. You may still find these headings in older catalogues.

When subordinate bodies are entered subordinately

24.13

Despite what I have just said, there are a number of cases where a subordinate body *does* have to be entered subordinately to another body.

When this happens, the subordinate part of the name is separated from the main heading by a full stop and space.

MARC:
$b for
subordinate part
of name

The examples in AACR2 always show the subordinate part in italic. You do not normally need to bother about this. In your automated system the MARC coding may or may not produce the italic automatically, and if it does not there is nothing you can do about it. If you are using a typewriter, you could underline the subordinate part of the name.

You will see that the various cases are listed as 'types' and numbered from 1 to 6. If you look at them you will see that in most cases the subordinate name would be meaningless, or almost so, if it were used on its own; it only has any meaning as part of a larger body. Sometimes you have to look for specific words.

Type 1

A name that *by definition* implies that the body is part of another. Most of these words are obvious and there is seldom any doubt; and remember that many such names are so common that they will occur as part of many different main corporate headings.

Type 2

A name that normally implies administrative subordination, *provided that* the name of the higher body is required for identification of the subordinate body.

This is rather harder to interpret, because it is often difficult to know whether a higher body is necessary for identification or not. The only advice I can give is that you need to consider your own catalogue or authority file and see what headings are already in use there.

Committees and Commissions can be a particular problem, because the authorized form chosen depends so much on whether the name is identifiable without the presence of the higher body's name.

Type 3

A name that is general in nature or that does no more than indicate a geographic, chronological, or numbered or lettered subdivision of the parent body.

Most of these are fairly clear, and there would be few problems were it not for that fact that at the end the rule says 'If in doubt, enter the body directly'. It always seems unsatisfactory to have a rule which says that if you are in doubt you should do the opposite of what the rule prescribes. I can only suggest that you remain free from doubt.

Type 4

A name that does not convey the idea of a corporate body. These are very unusual. Obviously it only applies if a higher body is relevant, otherwise you would add something in parentheses to the heading.

Type 5

A name of a university faculty, school, college, institute, laboratory, etc., that *simply* indicates a particular field of study. The operative word here is 'simply'. If the department is one of those that have someone's name attached to them, then the name does not *simply* indicate its field of study, and this rule does not apply.

Example

(Fig. 4.8, p. 38: added entry)

```
University of Cambridge. Department of Land
Economy
```

Type 6

A name that includes the entire name of the higher related body. This is a strange rule, and it is often difficult to apply because it is not always easy to establish the correct name of the higher body.

You have to look at the exact name of the higher body. This explains the example

```
BBC Symphony Orchestra
```

because the correct heading for the BBC is not

```
✗ BBC
```

but

```
✔ British Broadcasting Corporation
```

which means that the name of the subordinate body does *not* include the whole of the name of the higher body.

As another example, Cambridge University Library is called Cambridge University Library. But the University of Cambridge is not called Cambridge University, which means that the name of the Library does *not* include the entire name of the higher body. This in turn means that the form of heading will be

```
Cambridge University Library
```

whereas the heading for the University itself is

```
University of Cambridge
```

As a contrary example consider the University of London Library. This *does* contain the whole of the name of the higher body, i.e. University of London, which means that the heading will be

```
University of London. Library
```

This seems rather inconsistent, and to help your users you should always make a cross-reference from the subordinated form, i.e.

```
University of Cambridge. Library
See Cambridge University Library
```

Direct or indirect subheading   24.14A

This rule is designed to cater for the possibility of more than one level of subordination. It allows you to miss out intermediate steps in the hierarchy provided that this does not lead to difficulty in identification.

Looking at the second example, you can see four levels of hierarchy. You can miss out the second ('Resources and Technical Services Division') but no more. It is likely that several of the subdivisions have or might have a Policy and Research Committee, and it is therefore essential to retain the third level, 'Cataloguing and Classification Section'.

Joint committees, commissions, etc.   24.15

A body which is made up of representatives from more than one body is entered under its own name.

This is perhaps obvious, but you might think from the previous rule that it would have to be subordinated to a higher body, and you would then wonder how to do this when more than one body is involved. This rule avoids the problem.

Government names   24.17

A government body is just a special kind of corporate body, which means that to a great extent the rules are similar to those for ordinary corporate bodies.

We need to consider two things:

* the name of the government itself, i.e. the name of the country or jurisdiction
* the name of any body which is subordinate to the government name.

Some kinds of materials are entered under the name of the government *alone*, but most require the name of a subordinate body also.

MARC:
110 1_

The name of the government

Usually this means the name of a country, such as

168

```
France
Great Britain
United States
```

but remember that a government can be more local, so that it may be a city, a province, a county, or any other unit of local government.

These names are dealt with in AACR2 Chapter 23.   **23**

Use an English form if one exists, provided that it is still in general use; otherwise use the language of the country concerned.   **23.2A1**
23.2B1

If variant names exist use the conventional name, rather than a longer, more formal one.   **24.3E1**

There is a problem with the heading

```
Great Britain
```

You will see that in AACR2 all the examples show   **24.18A,**
etc.

```
United Kingdom
```

instead. Technically, because we are talking about a jurisdiction rather than a geographical area, this is the correct form. 'Great Britain' has been the term used for many years in both Britain and the USA, and when AACR2 was issued neither of the national libraries was inclined to change. It is likely therefore that most catalogues that you will see will use this heading.

Additions to names   **23.4,**
24.6

If necessary to distinguish between identical names, make appropriate additions.

It is beyond the scope of this book to deal adequately with such additions, because you need to see a very large number of examples. In practice you should seldom need to construct such headings from scratch.

Subordinate government bodies   **24.17A**

We start with a general rule, which says that, with certain exceptions which follow, a body created or controlled by a government is entered directly under its own name. If you compare this with the rule about subordinate bodies in general you will see that it makes sense because it means that provided that it has its own name you do not need to know whether a body is created or controlled by the government.

When you look at the examples, however, you will see that the kinds of name which are entered directly are those which are very specific and likely to be unique. They exclude, especially, government departments, because those are included in the list of certain types which *are* entered subordinately to the name of the government.

Government agencies entered subordinately 24.18A

We now come to a list of types of government body which are entered subordinately to the name of the government. This is very similar to the list of Types which we have just seen for ordinary corporate bodies, but it is longer because there are certain special provisions for government bodies.

Type 1

An agency with a name that by definition implies that it is part of another body. Again it is usually obvious that words like 'Department', 'Division', 'Section' and so forth will come under this rule. It includes all the well-known government departments with which we are familiar.

Example

(Fig. 5.5, p. 95: added entry or cross-reference)

```
Great Britain. Department of Transport
```

Type 2

An agency with a name containing a word that usually implies administrative subordination, *provided that* the name of the government is necessary for the identification of the agency.

This is rather like Type 2 of ordinary subordinate bodies, in that there is room for doubt, and this is always difficult. The final example is as it is because the name includes 'New Brunswick', which means that it must be obvious which jurisdiction it relates to. Other instances are not so clear.

Type 3

A name which is general in nature or does no more than indicate a geographic, chronological, or numbered or lettered subdivision.

It is pretty obvious when you look at these that this kind of word would be useless as a heading in its own right, and it therefore has to be subordinated to something else. But again the rule is spoilt by the final instruction, which in effect says, if in doubt do the opposite.

Type 4

A name which does not convey the idea of a corporate body. This again is straightforward after seeing the rule for ordinary subordinate bodies.

Type 5
We now move on to some different types which are specific to government bodies. These cover the names of government bodies which are not actually called 'Department', and therefore do not fall under Type 1. The commonest words in English are 'Ministry' and 'Office'.

Type 6
A legislative body. Note that this can include city councils and any kind of body which has the power to make legislation.

Type 7
A court.

Type 8
A principal service of the armed forces of a government. This is perhaps rather unexpected, but most general libraries are unlikely to have much material that falls under this rule. For further subdivisions see **24.24**.

24.24

Type 9
A head of state or head of government. This is a special kind of heading which is used on occasions when such an office-holder issues some statement in his or her official capacity.

24.18
Type 9
24.20

Type 10
An embassy, consulate, etc.

Type 11
A delegation to an international or intergovernmental body.

Direct or indirect subheading
This rule is parallel to the one for ordinary subordinate bodies, and most of its provisions are the same.

24.19

You must note, however, that for names of legislative bodies this rule does not apply, as it is overridden by another. In these cases you *do include* the intermediate level of the hierarchy. This results in

24.21

    ✔ United Kingdom. <u>Parliament. House of Commons</u>

not

    ✘ United Kingdom. <u>House of Commons</u>

as you might expect from the general rule about missing out intermediate steps in the division.

Government officials and heads of state 24.20

You start with the name of the country, and then add the appropriate subdivision. The arrangement is then chronological, according to the 24.20B1 dates during which the office was held.

Notice that in the case of King/Queen you use the term 'Sovereign', which does not change.

Courts 24.23

Courts are entered subordinately to the jurisdiction to which they refer.

Armed forces 24.24

I will not go through these rules, which you are unlikely to need often. Just be aware that they exist.

The remainder of AACR2 Chapter 24 deals with various other special kinds 24.25– of corporate body which are outside the scope of this book and very seldom 24.27 needed in most general libraries.

9 Authority control

What is authority control?

Authority control is not mentioned specifically in AACR2, but it is implied in the sections dealing with forms of name. It is the process whereby a library or cataloguing agency establishes authorized forms of name for *access points* and ensures that they are used consistently for all occurrences of such names.

It applies not only to names; it can be used for:

- personal names
- names of corporate bodies (of all kinds)
- uniform titles
- series
- subject headings.

(Subject headings are not covered in this book.) The main thing to notice is that it concerns the kinds of *access point* that may occur in more than one item. Although it can apply to uniform titles, it does not usually apply to ordinary titles, because they are so much more various.

Its main purpose is to assist retrieval by ensuring that all items that have an entry under a particular heading use the *same form* of the heading, so that, for example, all works of a particular author are brought together.

It also provides a means of ensuring that cross-references are consistently made, so that a user who looks for a name under the 'wrong' form will be directed to the 'right' one. This can range from a compound surname, where the user may be uncertain of the form of entry, to a government department, where the leading term in the heading will be the name of the jurisdiction.

Cross-references can be of 'see' or 'see also' form.

Why have authority control?

When computers were first introduced into cataloguing it used to be said – and it is still sometimes said now – that there was no need for

26

authority control, on the grounds that, by free-text searching, the user can retrieve any combination of desired words from *within the catalogue record*. Even if this were possible – and it is still not so in most OPACs – it would not solve the problem of authors who use different forms of their name in different works.

Nor would it help in the case of very common names, such as John Smith. AACR2 requires that such names are carefully differentiated, so that catalogue users can find just the one they want without having to wade through a lot of irrelevant records. They are usually differentiated by adding dates of birth and/or death, which is information that would hardly appear naturally in a catalogue description.

It would also be very unhelpful in those cases where one person's name is part of another person's, longer, name. For example, everyone has heard of Leonardo da Vinci. But fewer people know that later there was an Italian composer called Leonardo Vinci (1690–1730). Imagine trying to find Leonardo Vinci in a system where you could only search on words in the description. You would inevitably retrieve all the items containing Leonardo da Vinci as well.

Free text searching would certainly not provide for the collocative function of a catalogue in the case of authors who have changed their name. It would not provide for separate bibliographic identities. These are aspects which should be carefully brought together through a system of authority control, with the automatic production of cross-references.

How do you do authority control?

Until fairly recently it was unusual for most libraries to maintain separate authority files; the catalogue itself was its own authority file. You checked the names in the catalogue before you created the headings for the item you were cataloguing.

Nowadays, most library management systems include an authority control utility as part of their cataloguing module, which means that the whole process can be automated. This process should include the production of cross-references from variant forms of name, and should also provide for bulk changes when it is discovered that a name has to be altered in several separate catalogue records.

If authority control is not in operation locally, it is probably normal practice to check forms of name in an external authority file. Now that the Library of Congress authorities are available on the web this is easily accessible (http://authorities.loc.gov) and the examples in this chapter are all taken from this.

In recent years there have been moves towards the internationalization of authority records, so that the national libraries of different countries can use the same authority files. The Anglo-American Authority File has been developed by both the British Library and the Library of Congress, so that in future, in theory, they should be using the same forms of name.

None of this implies, however, that every library now has a perfect system of authority control. Most libraries' catalogues have been built up over a long period, and contain records from a variety of sources, most of them added at a time when it was not feasible to impose authority control upon them. Most catalogues are therefore far from perfect as regards forms of name.

Structure of an authority record

There is no international standard for authority control in the same way as AACR2 is a standard for cataloguing. There is, however, a MARC format for it, and many systems, including the Library of Congress, use this for their authority records.

There are three main pieces of information that need to be recorded in an authority record:

- the form of name which is authorized to be used
- variant forms of name (possibly a considerable list) from which cross-references should be made to the authorized form
- the sources of information used to establish the authorized form.

Let us look at these in turn.

MARC:
100 personal
110 corporate
111 conference

Authorized form of name

Clearly this will be the heading for the authority record, and it will consist of the name in the form required by AACR2, which is the authorized form to be used. It should follow exactly the same conventions for punctuation and capitalization.

In those cases where more than one form of name is authorized, there will be more than one authority record, with cross-references between them.

Looking at Fig. 9.1 (overleaf) we can see that the authorized form of name to be used is

```
Tonkin, Jim
```

```
LC Control Number: nb 91075586
       HEADING: Tonkin, Jim
            000  00406nz 2200145n 450
            001  4942672
            005  19990921051644.0
            008  911230n| acannaabn |a aaa c
            010  ___ |a nb 91075586
            035  ___ |a (DLC)nb 91075586
            040  ___ |a Uk |b eng |c Uk
            100  10 |a Tonkin, Jim
            400  10 |a Tonkin, J. W. |q (Jim W.)
            670  ___ |a The book of Hereford, 1975. |b t.p. (Jim Tonkin)
            670  ___ |a Herefordshire, 1977: |b t.p. (J.W. Tonkin)
```

Fig. 9.1

MARC:
4— for 'see' references
5— for 'see also' references

Variant forms of name

Here we list any other versions of the name which may have been used. Depending on the nature of the name, these may require *see* or *see also* cross-references to the authorized form.

In Fig. 9.1 we see that Jim Tonkin has also written a book in which he calls himself J. W. Tonkin, and a 'see' cross-reference is therefore made from this, using the 400 field.

The Alan Evans of *Rabbit hutches and postage stamps* fame (Fig. 4.8, p. 38) has written a number of other works, usually calling himself Alan W. Evans. Accordingly, the form

```
Evans, Alan W.
```

is used in the authority record (Fig. 9.2), and there ought to be a 'see' reference (400 field) from the other form, though this does not appear in our example.

A different situation is shown in Fig. 9.3. Barbara Vine is the name used by Ruth Rendell for some of her books (separate bibliographic identities). Because both names are legitimately used, there is a pair of similar records, with the alternative in each record going in the 500 field, which generates a 'see also' reference to the other name.   **22.2B2**

The same thing applies in the case of heads of state, popes, etc., who may write under both their personal and their 'official' names.   **21.4D1**

Sometimes a writer uses several pseudonyms, and Fig. 9.4 (p. 178) shows an example of this.

Fig. 9.5 (p. 179) shows cross-references from the various alternative forms of name that might be found for a title of nobility.

```
HEADING: Evans, Alan W.
    000  00510cz 2200169n 450
    001  1913180
    005  19890411170242.0
    008  801223n| acannaab |n aaa
    010  ___ |a n 80148891
    035  ___ |a (DLC)n 80148891
    040  ___ |a DLC |c DLC |d DLC
    100  10 |a Evans, Alan W.
    670  ___ |a His The economics of ... 1973.
    670  ___ |a His No room! No room! 1988: |b t.p. (Alan Evans; prof. of
              Environmental Economics, Univ. of Reading) p. 11 (b. 1938, Surrey)
    678  ___ |a b. 1939
    952  ___ |a RETRO
    953  ___ |a xx00 |b ea12
```

Fig. 9.2

MARC:
670

Sources of information

It is very important to record information about *why* the established form is the correct one, and details of where any supplementary information came from. This may include such details as information obtained from the publisher or from the author.

It will also usually give details of one or more of the author's works.

```
HEADING: Rendell, Ruth, 1930-
    000  00621cz 2200193n 450
    001  3751772
    005  20011127065830.0
    008  790705n| acannaabn |a aaa
    010  ___ |a n 79056533 |z n 85346076 |z sh 89003280
    035  ___ |a (OCoLC)oca00289626
    040  ___ |a DLC |b eng |c DLC |d DLC |d OCoLC
    053  _0 |a PR6068.E63
    100  1_ |a Rendell, Ruth, |d 1930-
    500  1_ |a Vine, Barbara, |d 1930-
    670  ___ |a Her From Doon with death, 1964.
    670  ___ |a Her A dark-adapted eye, 1986: |b CIP t.p. (Barbara Vine)
    670  ___ |a Info. from pub., 1/28/86 |b (Barbara Vine is pseud. used by Ruth
              Rendell)
    952  ___ |a RETRO
    953  ___ |a xx00 |b bd16
```

Fig. 9.3

```
HEADING: Ranney, Maurice William, 1934-
    000  00605cz 2200205n 450
    001  514731
    005  19890920074828.5
    008  801007n| acannaab |a aaa
    010  __ |a n 80126185
    035  __ |a (DLC)n 80126185
    040  __ |a DLC |c DLC |d DLC
    100  10 |a Ranney, Maurice William, |d 1934-
    400  10 |a Johnson, Keith, |d 1934-
    400  10 |a McDermott, John, |d 1934-
    400  10 |a Palmer, John W., |d 1934-
    400  10 |a Ranney, M. W. |q (Maurice William), |d 1934-
    400  10 |a Ranney, M. William |q (Maurice William), |d 1934-
    670  __ |a His Alkali metal phosphates, 1969.
    952  __ |a RETRO
    953  __ |a xx00 |b kb01
```

Fig. 9.4

Until an author has become very well known this is usually the only way of verifying that one is actually dealing with the same person, because many books give details of other works by the same author. Figs. 9.1–9.5 all show examples where titles of works are given in the authority record. Fig. 9.5 also shows the use of an external source of information (*Debrett's*).

Personal names

We have already looked at the rules for forms of heading for personal names (Chapter 7). How do you go about putting these rules into practice?

1. The first thing is to check the authority file to see whether the name is already there.
2. If it is not, and there is clearly no other name that might be of the same person, you can add it without more ado.
3. Make an authority record including the details of the item you are cataloguing. If there is any information in the item about the person's date of birth, job, affiliation, or anything else that might be useful, such as a list of other publications, include this.

This is relatively straightforward so far. The problem arises if *either*

```
HEADING: Cranbrook, Gathorne Gathorne-Hardy, Earl of, 1933-
      000  01138cz 2200253n 450
      001  1446375
      005  20000422064820.0
      008  801218n| acannaabn |a aaa
      010  __ |a n 80138789
      035  __ |a (OCoLC)oca00519037
      040  __ |a DLC |b eng |c DLC |d DLC |d MiU |d MiU |d OCoLC
      100  1_ |a Cranbrook, Gathorne Gathorne-Hardy, |c Earl of, |d 1933-
      400  1_ |w nna |a Medway, Gathorne Gathorne-Hardy, |c Lord, |d 1933-
      400  1_ |a Gathorne-Hardy, Gathorne, |c Earl of Cranbrook, |d 1933-
      400  1_ |a Hardy, Gathorne Gathorne-, |c Earl of Cranbrook, |d 1933-
      400  1_ |a Cranbrook, |c Earl of, |d 1933-
      400  1_ |a Medway, |c Lord, |d 1933-
      670  __ |a His Mammals of Borneo, 1965.
      670  __ |a Smythies, B. E. The birds of Borneo, 1981: |b t.p. (Earl of Cranbrook)
               p. iv ((M.) Lord Medway, chgd to (C.) Earl of Cranbrook)
      670  __ |a Debrett's |b (listed under Cranbrook, Earl of (Gathorne-Hardy): sons
               living: Gathorne (Lord Medway) b. 6-20-33)
      670  __ |a His Mammals of South-East Asia, 1991: |b t.p. (Earl of Cranbrook)
      670  __ |a Robinson, H.C. Birds of the Malay Penninsula, 1976: |b v.5, t.p. (Lord
               Medway)
      952  __ |a RETRO
      953  __ |a xx00 |b ta01
```

Fig. 9.5

- the new item bears a form of name which is slightly different from, but appears from the context to be for the same person as, a name which is already in the authority file; *or*
- the new item bears a name which is already in the authority file, but which apparently relates to a completely different person.

In the first case, the correct procedure is to follow AACR2 rule **22.3A1**. This involves checking the form of name which has been used in each of the author's previous works and establishing what is the correct form of name. You would do this by looking at the statements of responsibility in the descriptions.

If necessary the authority record should be changed, and a universal change effected in the catalogue headings.

In practice, this seems seldom to occur. What happens is that the form of name in the authority file is regarded as 'correct' come what may, and that form is then used for the new work.

22.3A1

This is clearly what happened in the case of the name in Fig. 9.1, and because both books predate AACR2 there is nothing wrong with this as it was the policy at the time. But under the current rules what should happen is that the original form is changed to

```
Tonkin, J. W.
```

because there is an equal number of works under each form, and therefore the latest takes precedence.

What do you do in the second case? There may be some information in the book referring to other works by the same author, and this may enable you to connect this name with a different form of it.

Normally, however, this does not happen. What happens next depends on what facilities you have available, and how much time you are prepared to devote to establishing forms of name.

If you are very lucky there may be a statement in the book telling you when the author was born. This is rare, but it is not unknown, and is relatively common in the case of artists' works.

Otherwise you need to try to find out a date of birth. Don't forget directories and reference books, which may yield results if you can get a hint of the kind of book to try. The better known the person, obviously the easier it is to find out more details.

The normal ways of finding out more are to write to the publisher or to the author and ask. The national libraries do, or used to do, this, but it is seldom feasible for an individual library to take on this task.

The practicality of the situation is that if you cannot find any way of differentiating the two names you will have to leave them identical and hope that further information comes to light in due course.

Corporate bodies

It is perhaps more likely that there will be more than one form of name when dealing with a corporate body than it is with an individual. For example, there are so many acronyms in use that it is normal to make cross-references from (or to) those.

In addition, organizations probably change their names more often than individuals.

There are two ways of making cross-references between names for organizations that have changed their name.

1. Simple cross-references

This is the easiest, as you simply provide 'see also' cross-references between the names and leave it to the catalogue user to work out why.

Example

> **Library Association** <u>see also</u> Chartered
> Institute of Library and Information
> Professionals
>
> **Chartered Institute of Library and**
> **Information Professionals** <u>see also</u> Library
> Association
>
> **Institute of Information Scientists** <u>see also</u>
> Chartered Institute of Library and
> Information Professionals
>
> **Chartered Institute of Library and**
> **Information Professionals** <u>see also</u> Institute
> of Information Scientists

This provides simple cross-references to and from the names of the organizations which became the Chartered Institute of Library and Information Professionals. It does not tell the user anything, or explain the relationship.

In many cases this kind of cross-reference is quite adequate.

2. *Explanatory cross-references*   24.1C1

This involves writing a potted history explaining the changes of name. In some cases it may involve several changes. It is much more useful for the catalogue user, and it may be the only way of dealing with complicated changes or with names that are not unique and require some explanation.

Example

> **Chartered Institute of Library and**
> **Information Professionals**
>
> In 2002 the Library Association and the
> Institute of Information Scientists merged to
> form the Chartered Institute of Library and
> Information Professionals.
>
> Works by these organizations are entered
> under the name used at the time of
> publication.

A similar explanation would be provided under the heading for each of the other two organizations.

Uniform titles
The authority file will keep a record of all the works which have a uniform title main entry. Items by individual authors that need uniform titles will be recorded in separate authority records under the authors' names.

Series
These are much more straightforward, as they do not normally involve much research.

The important thing is that, in addition to the form which is to be used for the entry point, you keep a record of all the forms in which the series statement has appeared in items. This is because you may need to make changes if a new form begins to predominate.

Also keep a record of whether you are including volume numbers in your added entries.

10 Uniform titles

The two types of uniform title

The term 'uniform title' can be confusing, because in AACR2 it is used in two different senses. These are called

- uniform title
- collective title.

This means that collective titles are just a particular kind of uniform title, but unfortunately there is no special name for the first (and *main*) kind of uniform title. The distinction is that a uniform title (in the first sense) refers to an *individual work*, whereas a collective title is used in relation to a collection or selection of more than one work.

To try to avoid confusion I shall refer to the latter as 'collective title' **25.1A** throughout this chapter, which means that 'uniform title' refers to the first kind only. In AACR2 'collective titles' are sandwiched in the middle of Chapter 25, but I am leaving them to the end because I think this makes more sense.

Both kinds, 'uniform titles' and 'collective titles', are unusual in two respects:

- they are *optional*
- they are concerned with filing.

The fact that they are optional means that an individual library can decide how far, if at all, it wishes to use uniform titles in its catalogue. It may decide to use them for some kinds of work but not for others; we shall look at possible examples of this later. If your library does not need to use them you can ignore this chapter altogether.

The reason that I think the second point is unusual is that AACR2 has nothing to say about filing, and indeed says nothing about the practical application of uniform titles or about the intended results that their presence should achieve in a catalogue.

Uniform titles for individual works

A uniform title is basically something very simple: it is a standardized title for an item which may have appeared under a variety of different titles. This means that, unlike the title proper, it is *not* copied from the chief source of information: it is something inserted by the cataloguer when required. The uniform title thus enhances the *collocating* function of the catalogue, by bringing together individual works regardless of the actual title on the title page.

This makes two assumptions about the catalogue:

* that the uniform title will 'work', and have this effect
* that under an individual author there is some sensible alphabetical sequence for the individual works.

In many online catalogues, sadly, neither of these assumptions holds good.

Most items have no need of uniform titles at all because they are published once, under a single title, and never become known by any other title. But there are certain kinds of work for which a uniform title can be useful, and we shall look at these in due course.

MARC:
130 for main entry, 240 otherwise

Another point to notice is that, just as the title proper may or may not be the main entry for a work, so this kind of uniform title may or may not be the main entry.

Main uses of uniform titles

Before going on to look at the actual form of uniform titles it will be useful to look at the kinds of work that may require them. There are several kinds of work where a uniform title may be thought appropriate, but the commonest occurrences can be described in two simple groups:

* works that have been known by more than one title
* certain special kinds of work, such as laws and sacred scriptures.

We can further subdivide each of these two groups. Let us look at the first group first, and divide them into

* translations
* other works.

Translations

I am dealing with these first because in many ways they are the simplest to understand. Many works are translated from their original language into another one. The purpose of assigning a uniform title is to enable the translation to appear next to the original language edition in the alphabetical sequence in a catalogue.

Note that this is *not* like a parallel title (see pp. 34–5), where *both* titles must appear at the same time on the title page.

Think about whether such a uniform title would be useful in your catalogue. If you have a large collection of foreign literature, for example, and often have translations of individual works, it may well be useful to use uniform titles. On the other hand, if most of your foreign-language literature is translated into English and you have relatively little in the original languages, you may feel that it would be positively unhelpful to the catalogue users to insert uniform titles.

Some libraries choose to use uniform titles for works of literature but not for, say, scientific works, where it is less likely that library users would be interested in the original language. It all depends on the nature of your collection, which is why so much flexibility is allowed. Make sure that you establish a policy, record it and keep to it.

The uniform title for a translated work will consist of the title in the *original* language, followed by a full stop, space and then the language of the *translation*. Remember to get this the right way round; the whole purpose of the uniform title is to allow the item to appear next to the *original* language.

25.5C1

Example

(Fig. 10.1, overleaf)

```
Febvre, Lucien

[Apparition du livre. English]

The coming of the book : the impact of
printing 1450-1800 / Lucien Febvre, Henri-
Jean Martin ; translated by David Gerard ;
edited by Geoffrey Nowell-Smith and David
Wootton. - London : Verso, 1984. - 378 p. ;
21 cm. - Translation of: L'apparition du
livre. - English ed. originally published:
London : NLB, 1976
```

Notice the omission of the initial article ('L') (see below, p. 189).

25.2C1

Other kinds of uniform title

So much for translations, which are quite easy to understand. The other kind of uniform title for individual works is rather harder to pin down. The easiest way to think of examples is to look at the works of

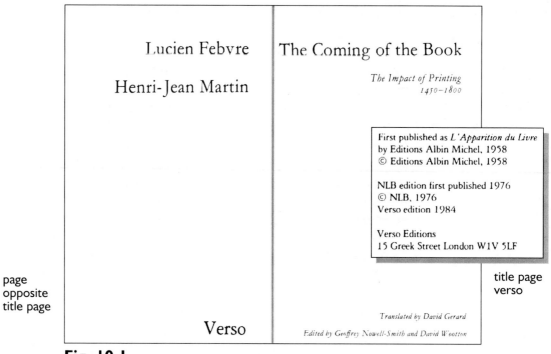

Fig. 10.1

Shakespeare, where you may find all kinds of different versions of the same title appearing on the title pages of different editions. For example, all these are legitimate titles proper for various editions of *Hamlet*:

> *The first quarto edition of Shakespeare's Hamlet*
> *Hamlet*
> *Hamlet, Prince of Denmark*
> *Shakespeare's Hamlet*
> *The tragedie of Hamlet, Prince of Denmarke*
> *The tragedy of Hamlet*
> *The tragicall historie of Hamlet Prince of Denmarke*
> *William Shakespeare's Hamlet*

If someone is trying to find all the editions of *Hamlet* in a given library or collection, it is helpful if they can be arranged so as to file together. This is achieved by means of a uniform title. Look also at the examples in AACR2. You can see three different examples of *Martin Chuzzlewit* by Charles Dickens, and each has a different version of the

25.2A

title on its title page. The uniform title will bring them together.

Notice that if the title page title is the same as the uniform title, the uniform title may be omitted.

When to use a uniform title

Beginners are sometimes puzzled as to *what kind of work* might need a uniform title of this kind. Always remember that *most works do not need uniform titles at all*. It is almost inconceivable that you would ever need to construct a uniform title of this kind for a *new* work. It needs to have time to become known by some other form of title, which means that as a rule of thumb you can assume that this kind of uniform title is restricted to really well-known 'classics' of various kinds, such as the works of Shakespeare and Dickens which we have already seen.

Do not use a uniform title for what is actually a revised edition in the same language, that happens to have been given a different title from the original. In this case put the original title in a note.

25.2B

Form of uniform title

Remember that by definition we are inventing the uniform title, or at least getting it from reference sources, rather than copying it from something in the item. This means that it is normally enclosed in square brackets because it is something that is *not there*. Usually it appears on a separate line, between the main author heading, if there is one, and the title proper. If there is no author heading, it will appear above the title proper, and in this case you have the option of using square brackets or not, as you prefer.

25.2A

It is unlikely that you will need to think about things like square brackets in an automated system, because the system should deal with things like that for you.

What people sometimes find difficult is knowing *how to decide what form of title to use*. This can sometimes be hard, but you should usually choose the *shortest possible* form that is not ambiguous. Think of how we would usually refer to the work. If necessary look in reference books, such as *The Oxford companion to English literature*. And of course if your library has a comprehensive system of authority control you should find the established form there already if you have used it before.

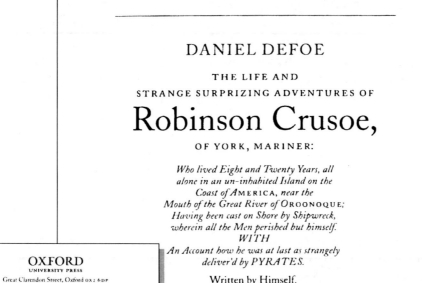

OXFORD WORLD'S CLASSICS

DANIEL DEFOE

THE LIFE AND
STRANGE SURPRIZING ADVENTURES OF

Robinson Crusoe,

OF YORK, MARINER:

*Who lived Eight and Twenty Years, all
alone in an un-inhabited Island on the
Coast of AMERICA, near the
Mouth of the Great River of OROONOQUE;
Having been cast on Shore by Shipwreck,
wherein all the Men perished but himself.*
WITH
*An Account how he was at last as strangely
deliver'd by PYRATES.*

Written by Himself.

WITH AN INTRODUCTION BY

J. M. COETZEE

OXFORD
UNIVERSITY PRESS

OXFORD
UNIVERSITY PRESS

Great Clarendon Street, Oxford OX2 6DP

Oxford University Press is a department of the University of Oxford.
It furthers the University's objective of excellence in research, scholarship,
and education by publishing worldwide in

Oxford New York

Athens Auckland Bangkok Bogotá Buenos Aires Calcutta
Cape Town Chennai Dar es Salaam Delhi Florence Hong Kong Istanbul
Karachi Kuala Lumpur Madrid Melbourne Mexico City Mumbai
Nairobi Paris São Paulo Singapore Taipei Tokyo Toronto Warsaw

and associated companies in Berlin Ibadan

Oxford is a registered trade mark of Oxford University Press
in the UK and in certain other countries

Published in the United States
by Oxford University Press Inc., New York

Introduction © J. M. Coetzee 1999

First published as an Oxford World's Classics hardback 1999

title page
verso

OXFORD WORLD'S CLASSICS

9

ROBINSON CRUSOE

half title
page

Fig. 10.2

188

Example
(Fig. 10.2, opposite)

Defoe, Daniel

[Robinson Crusoe]

The life and strange surprizing adventures of Robinson Crusoe, of York, mariner : who lived eight and twenty years … / written by himself ; Daniel Defoe ; with an introduction by J.M. Coetzee. - Oxford : Oxford University Press, 1999. - xi, 306 p. ; 17 cm. - (Oxford world's classics ; 9)

Omission of initial article
25.2C1

Whatever the purpose of the uniform title, if it starts with an article (definite or indefinite) then, whatever language it is in, you *must* omit it – even if, as may happen in German, this makes the next part of the title ungrammatical.

The uniform title only ever goes as far as the title proper; you do *not* include 'other title information'. But see below (p. 190) for part-titles.

It is unfortunate that both 130 and 240 have a filing indicator. This is a relic from the days before this rule. It should now *always* be set to 0.

Classical and Byzantine Greek works
25.4B1

These are an exception to the fact that the uniform title is normally in the original language. Presumably because most systems would have difficulty with Greek letters and also because classical Greek works tend to known by a variety of titles, in these cases you use the *English* title, if there is one, surprising though this may seem. If there is no English title, use a Latin one, and only failing this the Greek.

Additions to uniform titles
25.5

MARC:
130: no coding; just use parentheses.

The first of these really only applies in cases where the uniform title is the main entry, i.e. for certain anonymous works, and especially for periodical titles. In these cases you can add an explanation in parentheses, but this is comparatively rare.

25.5B1

MARC:
130 $l
240 $l

More common is the need to indicate the language *into which* an item has been translated. You do this by adding a full stop at the end of the uniform title, then a space and the language concerned.

Normally you might think this is obvious from the title proper, and of course it is, but for the sake of consistency, and to help users who might not recognize the language, it is useful to indicate it.

Notice that if the item you are dealing with is in two languages *and needs a uniform title*, you put both the languages, original language second if this applies.

Don't confuse this with the ordinary use of a parallel title. A uniform title is something quite different.

Parts of a work   25.6

Considering that AACR2 is not very helpful in dealing with multipart works, it is perhaps surprising to see this rule here.

In essence it tells you that if an individual part of a multipart work has a distinctive title of its own, you use that as the uniform title, rather than the multipart title.   25.6A1

Conversely, if the individual part is identified only by a general term (like 'volume', 'part', 'book', etc., and a number) you use the multipart title as the uniform title. This is advice which would be more generally applicable in deciding how to deal with multipart works generally, and it is a pity that it is relegated to this position, as it is not clear whether it is meant to be more widely applicable.   25.6A2

Special uses of uniform titles
Manuscripts   25.13A1

You may occasionally have to deal with a published edition of an anonymous manuscript, and this rule tells you how to construct a uniform title if you decide to use one.

This is probably a case where most libraries would wish to use a uniform title even if they have decided not to use them more generally, because the uniform title is almost like an author, without which you might be uncertain how the title would be entered. There have been many editions of the Dead Sea scrolls in recent years, and this would be applicable to them.

Laws, treaties, etc.   25.15A

This is another area where it is common for libraries to use a uniform title, because it is supposed to help the arrangement of collections of laws and individual laws in a catalogue.

Unfortunately, because of the stupidity of the rule, it is impossible to apply it in such a way as to achieve what uniform titles are meant to achieve.

For a collection of laws, unless they are all on a particular subject, you use the uniform title   25.15A1

        [Laws, etc.]

The usefulness of this is nullified by the fact that *individual* laws have   25.15A2 their uniform title put in in the same way, and in the same field in a MARC record. This means that the alphabetical sequence of individual law titles from A to Z is interrupted by the entries for collections which will all appear at L, because they all start with the word 'Laws'. Because AACR2 says nothing about filing, we cannot be certain of the intention of the rule, but it would be highly surprising if this were it.

Sacred scriptures

MARC:
130

Another category of work where uniform titles can be useful is sacred scriptures. Because they lack an author and may have a variety of different titles on the title page it is more convenient to enter them under a uniform title. This is another case where most libraries would probably choose to use one even if they do not do so for other purposes.

Again it is disappointing that very few OPACs are capable of producing a sensible display of titles under a heading such as **Bible**. There are occasional exceptions to this, but it has usually required special software developments, which most libraries would not wish to undertake. Most libraries probably do not have enough editions of sacred works to regard it as a problem.

MARC:
130 $aBible
subfields:
$p (repeatable)
for subdivisions,
e.g. O.T.
$l for language
$k for selections

The Bible

25.18A

I do not intend to go through all the rules in AACR2 because they are largely self-explanatory. I will draw attention to three points only:

Selections

25.18A7

Notice that some selections are usually identified by their own title, and in these cases you use that title itself as the uniform title, rather than a subdivision of the **Bible** uniform title, e.g.

```
Ten commandments
```

MARC:
$s

Versions

25.18A11

In addition to language, you can specify the *version*, which is a way of specifying the particular translation that you are dealing with.

Although many other works of literature have also been translated more than once, such translations are not so many that this provision needs to be made for them.

The
NIV
STUDY
BIBLE

NEW INTERNATIONAL VERSION

with *Study Notes and References,*
Concordance and Maps

The NIV Study Bible

The Holy Bible, New International Version
Copyright © 1973, 1978, 1984 by International Bible Society

The NIV Study Bible
Copyright © 1985 by The Zondervan Corporation

Anglicisation © 1987 by Hodder & Stoughton Limited

This edition first published in Great Britain 1987

title page
verso

♟

HODDER & STOUGHTON
LONDON   SYDNEY   AUCKLAND   TORONTO

Fig. 10.3

Example

(Fig. 10.3, opposite)

> **Bible**. <u>English. New International</u>
>
> The NIV study Bible : New International
> Version : with study notes and references,
> concordance and maps. - London : Hodder &
> Stoughton, 1987. - xviii, 2145, 14 p. : 14
> maps ; 24 cm.

MARC:
$f

Year of publication 25.18A13

Another unique provision is that you should add the year of the edition at the end of the uniform title. This is not permitted for other literary works.

The fact that it is not permitted has never stopped the Library of Congress from using it with other works, and you may see this in their records.

MARC:
243 exists but
240 is normally
used.

Collective titles 25.8

We now move on to the other kind of uniform title, the *collective title*. 25.9

Don't confuse this use of the term 'collective title' with the one that appears elsewhere, meaning an 'overall title' for a whole book that contains more than one separate work. 1.1G1, 21.7

AACR2 says nothing about the purpose of collective titles, and does not properly explain the relationship of this kind to the ordinary uniform title. There is not even any explanation of the fact that they should do something special in filing.

The purpose of a collective title is again to assist filing, by causing certain kinds of collections of works to file at the beginning of the alphabet (under the author's name), before individual titles starting with A. It means that someone looking for any edition of the complete works of the author can find it easily without knowing whether it is called

> *The works of …*
> *The complete works of …*
> *The collected …*
> *…'s collected works*

etc., any of which would appear in a different place in an ordinary alphabetical sequence.

Unfortunately OPACs that are able to take account of collective titles are far to seek, which means that it is almost useless putting them in.

You might object that as most OPACs allow you to type the author's name in one box and 'works' in another you can probably find most of these things anyway. This is true, but it does not take account of editions that do not contain the word 'works' in their title.

We have seen that an ordinary uniform title can in some cases be the main entry for the item. This can *never* be the case with a collective title, which can *only* occur in relation to an individual author.

The other important thing to notice is that although (theoretically) uniform titles and collective titles have different MARC fields they are mutually exclusive, being essentially different kinds of the same thing. You can never have a collective title if you have already put the other kind of uniform title.

Complete works   25.8

In theory these collections should file first, and this would be achieved by special programming in a catalogue that was properly set up to implement collective titles. However, MARC 21 does not have any way of differentiating between different kinds of collective title, which means that it would be impossible to file them properly even if the catalogue software could do so.

You put

    [Works]

as a separate element between the main author heading and the title proper.

Selections   25.9

In a similar way you put

    [Selections]

on a separate line. 'Selections' may mean *either*

- items consisting of three or more works (which may or may not be in different forms); *or*
- items consisting of extracts, of which it is not necessary for any to be complete.

Other collections in a single form   25.10

If the author wrote works in more than one literary form, you should

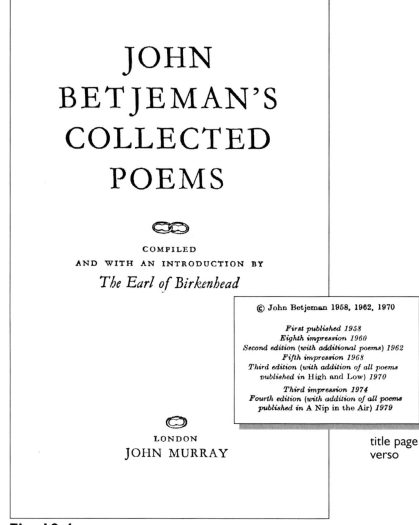

Fig. 10.4

specify which form is contained in the item. There is a list of possible terms, and these are inserted in the same way, e.g.

    [Plays]

Notice that if the collection you are dealing with contains only *some* of the author's works in that literary form, you should add

    . Selections

resulting in

    [Plays. Selections]

Note also that if the author wrote in *only one* literary form you do not use these terms at all, but instead use

        [Works]

or

        [Selections]

as appropriate, as in the previous examples.

Example
(Fig. 10.4, p. 195)

> **Betjeman, John**
>
> [Poems]
>
> John Betjeman's collected poems / compiled and with an introduction by the Earl of Birkenhead. - 4th ed. - London : John Murray, 1979. - xxxii, 427 p. ; 19 cm. - Previous ed.: 1970

Translations involving collective titles   25.11

It is of course perfectly possible to have a translation of a selection of works involving a collective title, and in this case the language is added in the same way as it was for uniform titles, e.g.

        [Short stories. Spanish. Selections]

Notice that in this case the language is specified first, before 'Selections'.

Bibliography

Arlis UK & Ireland, Cataloguing and Classification Committee (2000) *Art exhibition documentation in libraries: cataloguing guidelines*, Arlis.

Byrne, Deborah J. (1998) *MARC manual: understanding and using MARC records*, Libraries Unlimited.

Clack, Doris Hargrett (1990) *Authority control: principles, applications and instructions*, American Library Association.

Cutter, Charles Ammi (1904) *Rules for a dictionary catalog*, 4th ed., rewritten, Government Printing Office.

Hill, R. W. (1999) *Setting the record straight: a guide to the MARC format*, 3rd ed., British Library.

Library Association (1908) *Cataloguing rules: author and title entries*, compiled by committees of the Library Association and of the American Library Association, Library Association.

Library of Congress, Network Development and MARC Standards Office (2001) *MARC 21 concise format for bibliographic data*, Library of Congress, available at http://lcweb.loc.gov/marc/bibliographic/.

Lubetzky, Seymour (1953) *Cataloging rules and principles: a critique of the A.L.A. rules for entry and a proposed design for their revision*, Library of Congress.

Oddy, Pat (1996) *Future libraries, future catalogues*, Library Association Publishing.

Piggott, Mary (1988) *A topography of cataloguing: showing the most important landmarks, communications and perilous places*, Library Association Publishing.

Stephens, Andy (1994) *The history of the British National Bibliography 1950–1973*, British Library.

Turp, Stephen (1992) Guidelines on cataloguing off-air videorecordings, *Audiovisual Librarian*, **18** (2), 94–112.

Appendix: Catalogue records in MARC 21 format for the examples in this book

Notes

These records give the information required by AACR2 only. A full MARC record would contain other fields, such as coded information in the 008 field, subject access points, class-numbers and other things.

Forms of name: I have tried to provide reasonable forms of name for all access points, but have not attempted to achieve consistency with any single authority file. Notes on individual examples draw attention to particular problems.

Punctuation: I have not included end-of-field punctuation. In many systems you will be expected to include a full stop at the end of the field. In the case of series fields, I have assumed that the parentheses would be generated automatically.

Note area: I have not included notes of bibliographical references and indexes. It is not easy to do these consistently, and I believe them to be of doubtful value.

Fig. 4.1

```
100  1    $aHenig, Martin
245  14   $aThe art of Roman Britain / $cMartin Henig
260       $aLondon : $bBatsford, $c1995
300       $a224 p., [8] p. of plates : $b125 ill. (16 col.)
          ; $c25 cm.
```

Fig. 4.2

```
100  1    $aGorman, Martyn L.
245  14   $aThe natural history of moles / $cMartyn L.
          Gorman and R. David Stone
260       $aLondon : $bChristopher Helm, $c1990
```

```
300      $axiv, 138 p. : $bill. (some col.) ; $c24 cm.
490 0    $aChristopher Helm mammal series
700 1    $aStone, R. David
```

The series statement might equally be coded as 440.

Fig. 4.3

```
100 1    $aClifton, Robert T.
245 10   $aBarbs, prongs, points, prickers & stickers : $ba
         complete and illustrated catalogue of antique
         barbed wire / $cRobert T. Clifton
260      $aNorman [Okla.] : $bUniversity of Oklahoma Press,
         $cc1970
300      $axxi, 418 p. : $b992 ill. ; $c19 cm.
```

In this case I have included 'c' before the date to show that it is a copy-right date.

Fig. 4.4

```
100 1    $aTrimmer, John W.
245 10   $aHow to avoid huge ships, or, I never met a ship
         I liked / $cby John W. Trimmer
260      $aSeattle : $bJ.W. Trimmer, $cc1982
300      $axiii, 97 p. : $bill. ; $c22 cm.
```

Fig. 4.5

```
100 1    $aMcBride, Anne
245 10   $aWhy does my rabbit - ? / $cAnne McBride ; with
         drawings by Nina Bondarenko
260      $aLondon : $bSouvenir Press, $c1998
300      $a208 p. : $bill. ; $c22 cm.
```

Fig. 4.6

```
100 1    $aBeard, Henry
245 10   $aLatin for all occasions / $cby Henry Beard =
         Lingua Latina occasionibus omnibus / Henricus
         Barbatus scripsit
260      $aLondon : $bHarperCollins, $c1993
300      $axviii, 91 p. : $bill. ; $c21 cm.
500      $aFirst British ed.: London : Angus & Robertson,
         1991
```

Notice here that because 245 $a and $c cannot be repeated, there is no special coding for the parallel title or statement of responsibility.

Fig. 4.7

```
100 1   $aCranbrook, Gathorne Gathorne-Hardy, $cEarl of,
        $d1933-
245 10  $aRiches of the wild : $bland mammals of South-
        East Asia / $cEarl of Cranbrook ; with coloured
        plates by A.M. Hughes
260     $aSingapore ; $aOxford : $bOxford University
        Press, $c1987
300     $avii, 95 p., [12] p. of plates : $bill. (some
        col.), 2 maps ; $c20 cm.
440   0 $aImages of Asia
```

Fig. 4.8

```
100 1   $aEvans, Alan W.
245 10  $aRabbit hutches on postage stamps : $beconomics,
        planning and development in the 1990s / $cAlan
        Evans
260     $a[Cambridge?] : $bGranta Editions, $cc1990
300     $a25 p. ; $c21 cm.
490 1   $aThe 12th Denman lecture, 1990
500     $a"University of Cambridge, Department of Land
        Economy"
710 2   $aUniversity of Cambridge. $bDepartment of Land
        Economy
830   0 $aDenman lectures ; $v12
```

Fig. 4.9

```
100 1   $aSheldrake, Rupert
245 10  $aDogs that know when their owners are coming home
        : $band other unexplained powers of animals /
        $cRupert Sheldrake
260     $aLondon : $bHutchinson, $c1999
300     $axx, 300 p. : $bill. ; $c25 cm.
```

Fig. 4.10

```
245 00  $aMelchanolies [sic] of knowledge : $bliterature
        in the age of science / $cedited by Margery Arent
        Safir
246 3   $aMelancholies of knowledge
260     $aAlbany, N.Y. : $bState University of New York
        Press, $c1999
300     $ix, 205 p. ; $c23 cm.
440   4 $aThe margins of literature
700 1   $aSafir, Margery Arent
```

Fig. 4.11

```
100 1   $aHusain, B. M. C.
245 10  $aCheshire under the Norman earls : $b1066-1237 /
        $cby B.M.C. Husain ; cartography by A.G. Hodgkiss
260     $aChester : $bCheshire Community Council
        Publications Trust, $c1973
300     $axi, 142 p., [4] p. of plates : $bill., maps ;
        $c24 cm.
490 1   $aVolume four of a history of Cheshire
710 2   $aCheshire Community Council. $bPublications Trust
830  2  $aA history of Cheshire ; $vv. 4
```

Another way of dealing with the entry for the Cheshire Community Council would be to make a cross-reference from that name to the series title. This would enable anyone who searched under Cheshire Community Council to find all the volumes in this series.

Fig. 4.12

```
100 1   $aJohnson, Victoria M.
245 10  $aAll I need to know in life I learned from
        romance novels / $c[Victoria M. Johnson]
260     $aSanta Monica [Calif.] : $bGeneral Pub. Group,
        $cc1998
300     $a160 p. ; $c23 cm.
```

Fig. 4.13

```
245 00  $aBird census techniques / $cColin J. Bibby … [et
        al.] ; illustrated by Sandra Lambton, RSPB and
        Simon Mustoe
250     $a2nd ed.
260     $aLondon : $bAcademic Press, $c2000
300     $axvi, 302 p. : $bill., maps ; $c26 cm.
500     $aPrevious ed.: 1992
700 1   $aBibby, Colin
700 1   $aLambton, Sandra
700 1   $aMustoe, Simon
710 2   $aRoyal Society for the Protection of Birds
```

Fig. 4.14

```
100 1   $aFenwick, Helen
245 10  $aConstitutional & administrative law / $cHelen
        Fenwick
250     $a2nd ed.
260     $aLondon : $bCavendish, $c1995
300     $axvi, 365 p. ; $c22 cm.
```

```
490 0    $aThe Cavendish Q & A series
500      $aPrevious ed.: 1993
```

Fig. 4.15

```
100 1    $aBryson, Bill
245 14   $aThe lost continent : $btravels in small town
         America ; and, Neither here nor there : travels in
         Europe / $cBill Bryson
260      $aLondon : $bSecker & Warburg, $c1992
300      $a498 p. ; $c24 cm.
500      $aThe lost continent first published in Great
         Britain: 1989 - Neither here nor there first
         published in Great Britain: 1991
740 02   $aNeither here nor there
```

Fig. 4.16

```
100 1    $aRogers, W. V. H.
245 10   $aWinfield and Jolowicz on tort
250      $a14th ed. / $bby W.V.H. Rogers
260      $aLondon : $bSweet & Maxwell, $c1994
300      $alxxiv, 794 p. ; $c24 cm.
500      $aPrevious ed.: 1989
700 1    $aWinfield, Percy Henry, $d1878-1953. $tText-book
         of the law of tort
700 1    $aJolowicz, J. A. $q(John Anthony)
```

Notice the form of the name-title added entry, which is based on the original title of the book.

Fig. 4.17

```
245 00   $aCongestion charging : $bLondon Assembly scrutiny
         report
260      $aLondon : $bGreater London Authority, $c2000
300      $a1 v. in various pagings : $bcol. ill. ; $c30 cm.
490 0    $aReport ; $v1
710 2    $aGreater London Authority
```

Fig. 4.18

```
100 1    $aRyley, Michael
245 10   $aEmployment law for the construction industry /
         $cMichael Ryley and Edward Goodwyn ; Christopher
         Dering, consulting editor
260      $aLondon : $bThomas Telford, $c2000
300      $axiv, 157 p. ; $c22 cm.
490 0    $aMasons' guide
500      $aAt head of title: Masons
```

```
700 1  $aGoodwyn, Edward
700 1  $aDering, Christopher
710 2  $aMasons (Firm)
```

Fig. 5.1

```
111 2  $aInternational Pineapple Symposium $n(3rd : $d1998
       : $cPattaya, Thailand)
245 10 $aProceedings of the Third International Pineapple
       Symposium : $bPattaya, Thailand, 17-20 November
       1998 / $ceditors S. Subhadrabandhu, P. Chairidchai
260    $aLeuven : $bISHS, $c2000
300    $a341 p. : $bill. ; $c24 cm.
440 0  $aActa horticulturae ; $v529
700 1  $aSubhadrabandhu, S.
700 1  $aChairidchai, P.
710 2  $aInternational Society for Horticultural Science
```

Fig. 5.2

```
245 00 $aHomotopy theory and its applications : $ba
       conference on algebraic topology in honor of
       Samuel Gitler, August 9-13, 1993, Cocoyoc, Mexico
       / $cAlejandro Adem, R. James Milgram, Douglas C.
       Ravenel, editors
260    $aProvidence, R.I. : $bAmerican Mathematical
       Society, $cc1995
300    $aviii, 237 p. ; $c26 cm.
440  0 $aContemporary mathematics ; $v188
700 1  $aGitler, Samuel
700 1  $aAdem, Alejandro
700 1  $aRavenel, Douglas C.
700 1  $aMilgram, R. James
710 2  $aAmerican Mathematical Society
```

Another way of dealing with the entry for the American Mathematical Society would be to make a cross-reference to the series title instead (cf. 4.11).

The series has an ISSN, which could be included in $x of the series field. In this case the series would probably have to be coded as 490, because the added entry would not require the ISSN, and a separate 830 would need to be made.

Fig. 5.3

```
245 00   $aAdvanced polymer composites for structural
         applications in construction : $bproceedings of
         the first international conference, held at
         Southampton University, UK, on 15-17 April 2002 /
         $cedited by R.A. Shenoi, S.S.J. Moy, L.C. Hollaway
260      $aLondon : $bThomas Telford, $c2002
300      $a508 p. : $bill. ; $c25 cm.
700 1    $aShenoi, R. A.
700 1    $aMoy, S. S. J.
700 1    $aHollaway, L. C.
```

Fig. 5.4

```
110 2    $aChartered Institute of Library and Information
         Professionals
245 10   $aYearbook 2002-2003 / $cCILIP: the Chartered
         Institute of Library and Information Professionals
         ; compiled by Kathryn Beecroft
260      $aLondon : $bFacet, $c2003
300      $aviii, 456 p. ; $c25 cm.
500      $aPreviously published as: The Library Association
         yearbook
700 1    $aBeecroft, Kathryn
```

Fig. 5.5

```
110 1    $aGreat Britain. $bStanding Advisory Committee on
         Trunk Road Assessment
245 10   $aTrunk roads and the generation of traffic /
         $cthe Standing Advisory Committee on Trunk Road
         Assessment ; chairman D.A. Wood
260      $aLondon : $bHMSO, $c1994
300      $a242 p. : $bill., maps ; $c30 cm.
700 1    $aWood, D. A.
```

This book has 'The Department of Transport' at the head of the title. I have not made an access point for this, on the assumption that there would be a cross-reference in the form

```
Great Britain. Department of Transport. Standing Advisory
       Committee on Trunk Road Assessment
see
Great Britain. Standing Advisory Committee on Trunk Road
       Assessment
```

Although the abbreviation for 'Her Majesty's Stationery Office' is

'H.M.S.O.' with full stops, this publication actually shows 'HMSO' as an abbreviation. It therefore seems reasonable to copy it as it appears.

Fig. 5.6

```
110 1    $aGreat Britain. $bLaw Commission
245 10   $aDouble jeopardy and prosecution appeals :
         $breport on two references under section 3(1)(e)
         of the Law Commissions Act 1965 / $c the Law
         Commission ; presented to the Parliament of the
         United Kingdom by the Lord High Chancellor …
260      $aLondon : $bStationery Office, $c2001
300      $avi, 135 p. ; $c30 cm.
490 0    $aCm ; $v5048
490 0    $aLaw Com ; $vno. 267
```

In this case the book shows 'The Stationery Office', and there is no abbreviation for this.

Fig. 5.7

```
111 2    $aInternational Seaweed Symposium $n(16th : $d1998
         : $cCebu City, Philippines)
245 10   $aSixteenth International Seaweed Symposium :
         $bproceedings of the Sixteenth International
         Seaweed Symposium, held in Cebu City, Philippines,
         April 1998 / $cguest editors: Joanna M. Kain
         (Jones), Murray T. Brown & Marc Lahaye
260      $aDordrecht : $bKluwer Academic, $cc1999
300      $al, 668 p. : $bill. (some col.), maps, col. ports
         ; $c27 cm.
440 0    $aHydrobiologica ; $vv. 398/399
700 1    $aKain, Joanna M.
700 1    $aBrown, Murray T.
700 1    $aLahaye, Marc
```

Fig. 5.8

```
100 1    $aDe Grey, Roger
245 10   $aRoger de Grey
260      $a[London] : $bRoyal Academy of Arts, $c1996
300      $a96 p. : $bill. (chiefly col.) ; $c26 cm.
500      $aPublished on the occasion of an exhibition held
         11 July-22 Sept. 1996
710 2    $aRoyal Academy of Arts
```

Notice that the rules on abbreviations provide for September to be abbreviated, but July is written in full.

Fig. 5.9

```
110  2    $aBritish Museum
245 10    $aPre-Raphaelite drawings in the British Museum /
          $cJ.A. Gere
260       $aLondon : $bBritish Museum Press, $c1994
300       $a159 p., viii p. of plates : $b117 ill. (12 col.)
          ; $c28 cm.
700  1    $aGere, J. A.
```

Fig. 5.10

```
100  1    $aCornes, David L.
245 10    $aWinward Fearon on collateral warranties /
          $cDavid L. Cornes, Richard Winward
250       $a2nd ed.
260       $aOxford : $bBlackwell Science, $c2002
300       $ax, 338 p. : $bill. ; $c24 cm.
500       $aRevision of: Collateral warranties. Oxford : BSP
          Professional, 1990
700  1    $aWinward, Richard
710  2    $aWinward Fearon (Firm)
```

Fig. 5.11

```
100  1    $aBell, Florence
245 10    $aGreat expectations / $cCharles Dickens ; retold
          by Florence Bell
260       $aOxford : $bHeinemann ELT, $c1993
300       $a95 p. : $bill. ; $c20 cm.
490  0    $aHeinemann ELT guided readers. $pUpper level
700  1    $aDickens, Charles, $d1812-1870. $tGreat
          expectations
```

Fig. 5.12

```
100  1    $aPevsner, Nikolaus, $d1902-1983
245 10    $aLondon. $n1, $pThe cities of London and
          Westminster / $cby Nikolaus Pevsner
250       $a3rd ed. / $brevised by Bridget Cherry
260       $aLondon : $bPenguin, $c1973
300       $a756 p., [96] p. of plates : $bill., 4 maps ;
          $c19 cm.
440  4    $aThe buildings of England
500       $aPrevious ed.: 1962
700  1    $aCherry, Bridget
```

Fig. 5.13

```
100  1    $aSupperstone, Michael
```

```
245 14   $aThe Freedom of Information Act 2000 / $cMichael
         Supperstone, Timothy Pitt-Payne
260      $aLondon : $bButterworths, $c2001
300      $axii, 176 p. ; $c24 cm.
490 0    $aButterworths new law guides
500      $aIncludes the text of the Act
700 1    $aPitt-Payne, Timothy
710 1    $aGreat Britain. $tFreedom of Information Act 2000
```

Fig. 5.14
```
100 1    $aGraham-Dixon, Andrew
245 10   $aHoward Hodgkin / $cAndrew Graham-Dixon
260      $aLondon : $bThames and Hudson, $c1994
300      $a192 p. : $b114 ill. (96 col.) ; $c27 cm.
700 1    $aHodgkin, Howard
```

Fig. 5.15
```
100 0    $aDiana, $cPrincess of Wales, $d1961-1997
         $c(Spirit)
245 14   $aThe celestial voice of Diana : $bher spiritual
         guidance to finding love / $cchannelled by Rita
         Eide
260      $aFindhorn : $bFindhorn Press, $c1999
300      $a151 p. ; $c22 cm.
700 1    $aEide, Rita
```

The heading for the Spirit of Diana is based on that used by the
Library of Congress, but I have taken the liberty of adding the date of
death as, given the nature of the heading, it seemed rather peculiar not
to include it.

Fig. 6.1
```
100 1    $aKynaston, David
245 14   $aThe City of London. $nVolume IV, $pA club no
         more : 1945-2000 / $cDavid Kynaston
260      $aLondon : $bPimlico, $c2002
300      $a886 p., [16] p. of plates : $b27 ill. : $c24 cm.
500      $aOriginally published: London : Chatto & Windus,
         2001
```

Fig. 6.2
```
245 04   $aThe Renaissance : $b1550-1660 / $cedited by
         Gordon Campbell
260      $aBasingstoke : $bMacmillan Education, $c1989
300      $axxvii, 415 p. ; $c22 cm.
```

```
440   0   $aMacmillan anthologies of English literature ;
          $vv. 2
700   1   $aCampbell, Gordon
```

Fig. 6.3

```
245  00   $aOxford English dictionary additions series.
          $nVolume 1 / $cedited by John Simpson and Edmund
          Weiner
260       $aOxford : $bClarendon Press, $c1993
300       $axiii, 329 p. ; $c24 cm.
700   1   $aSimpson, J. A.
700   1   $aWeiner, E. S. C.
```

Fig. 8.1

```
110   2   $aCanadian Society for Computational Studies of
          Intelligence. $bConference $n(12th : $d1998 :
          $cVancouver, B.C.)
245  10   $aAdvances in artificial intelligence : $b12th
          Biennial Conference of the Canadian Society for
          Computational Studies of Intelligence, AI'98,
          Vancouver, BC, Canada, June 18-20, 1998 :
          proceedings / $c[editors Robert E. Mercer, Eric
          Neufeld]
260       $aBerlin ; $aLondon : $bSpringer, $c1998
300       $axii, 466 p. : $bill. ; $c24 cm.
440   0   $aLecture notes in computer science. $pLecture
          notes in artificial intelligence ; $v1418
700   1   $aMercer, Robert E.
700   1   $aNeufeld, Eric
```

Fig. 10.1

```
100   1   $aFebvre, Lucien
240  10   $aApparition du livre. $lEnglish
245  14   $aThe coming of the book : $bthe impact of
          printing 1450-1800 / $cLucien Febvre, Henri-Jean
          Martin ; translated by David Gerard ; edited by
          Geoffrey Nowell-Smith and David Wootton
260       $aLondon : $bVerso, $c1984
300       $a378 p. : $b2 maps ; $c21 cm.
500       $aTranslation of: L'apparition du livre. 1958.
          English ed. originally published: London : NLB,
          1976
700   1   $aMartin, Henri-Jean
700   1   $aNowell-Smith, Geoffrey
700   1   $aWootton, David
700   1   $aGerard, David
```

Fig. 10.2

```
100 1    $aDefoe, Daniel
240 10   $aRobinson Crusoe
245 14   $aThe life and strange surprizing adventures of
         Robinson Crusoe, of York, mariner : $bwho lived
         eight and twenty years … / $cwritten by himself ;
         Daniel Defoe ; with an introduction by J.M.
         Coetzee
260      $aOxford : $bOxford University Press, $c1999
300      $axi, 306 p. ; $c17 cm.
490 0    $aOxford world's classics ; $v9
700 1    $aCoetzee, J. M.
```

Fig. 10.3

```
130 0    $aBible. $lEnglish. $sNew International. $f1987
245 14   $aThe NIV study Bible : $bNew International
         Version : with study notes and references,
         concordance and maps
260      $aLondon : $bHodder & Stoughton, $c1987
300      $axviii, 2145, 14 p. : $b14 maps ; $c24 cm.
```

Fig. 10.4

```
100 1    $aBetjeman, John
240 10   $aPoems
245 10   $aJohn Betjeman's collected poems / $ccompiled and
         with an introduction by the Earl of Birkenhead
250      $a4th ed.
260      $aLondon : $bJohn Murray, $c1979
300      $axxxii, 427 p. ; $c19 cm.
500      $aPrevious ed.: 1970
```

Index

parallel titles 34–5
  contrasted with uniform titles 34, 190
  notes 81
  and statements of responsibility 52–3
parentheses
  in corporate names 154
  for series area 75
Paris Conference on Cataloguing Principles
      (1961) 8
Parliament, heading 171–2
parts of work (*see also* multipart works)
  uniform titles 190
personal authors *see* authors
personal names
  additions to 148, 151
  authority control 178–80
  change of 140
  choice of form 137–41
  compound 142–5
  distinguishing identical 149–51
  entry element 141–2
  forms of address omitted from statement of
        responsibility 50–1
  prefixes 144–5
  surnames 142–5
  as title proper 33
  variation in fullness 140
phrase, as heading 147–8
Physical description area 68–75
  summary 75
place names (*see also* countries; government
        names)
  added to corporate names 158–9
  in conference headings 163
  with titles of nobility 146
place of publication 57–61
  additions 58–9
  multiple 59–60
  not shown 60–1
plates 70–1
popes, form of name 147
prefixes to surnames 144–5
printers, ignored 57
printing, date of 67
'prominently'
  defined 15
  statements of responsibility 44
pseudonyms
  heading 139
  separate bibliographic identities 139–40
  shared 109

publication details, fictitious 23
Publication, distribution, etc. area 57–68
  dissertations 84
  summary 68
publishers 61–5
  lack of 65
  multiple 65
  omissions from statement 63
  same as author 65
punctuation 8–9, 21–2
  full stops 44
  illustrative matter 71
  imposed by AACR2 26–7
  MARC records 19, 21
  not transcribed 26, 31, 36
  other title information 36
  parallel title 34
  Publication, distribution, etc. area 57
  Series area 75
  statements of responsibility 41, 44
    Edition area 54
  subseries 79

quotations, in notes 80

recordings, place of publication 61
references *see* cross-references
related works 122–3
religious orders, names 157
reprints 56, 57
  date 67
reproductions 57
  art works 118–19
revised editions
  description 54–6
  entry 112–14
  and uniform titles 187
roman numerals
  converted to arabic 65
  pagination 70
royalty *see* monarchs

sacred scriptures
  entry 123
  uniform titles 191–3
saints, form of name 147, 148–9
scale, cartographic materials 56
scope notes 81
selections, collective title 194–6
semicolon, spacing around 22
separate bibliographic identities 139–40